Journey to Jerusalem

Steps on the Road to Your Soul

Mark A. Villano

Collegeville, Minnesota

www.litpress.org

1   2   3   4   5   6   7   8   9

Library of Congress Cataloging-in-Publication Data

Names: Villano, Mark A., author.
Title: Journey to Jerusalem : steps on the road to your soul / Mark A. Villano.
Description: Collegeville, Minnesota : Liturgical Press, 2020. | Includes bibliographical references. | Summary: "A resource for personal prayer using Scripture, personal stories, and reflections to invite readers to examine their lives as disciples of Jesus"— Provided by publisher.
Identifiers: LCCN 2019055226 (print) | LCCN 2019055227 (ebook) | ISBN 9780814688113 (paperback) | ISBN 9780814688359 (epub) | ISBN 9780814688359 (mobi) | ISBN 9780814688359 (pdf)
Subjects: LCSH: Spiritual life—Meditations. | Lent—Meditations.
Classification: LCC BV4832.3 .V543 2020 (print) | LCC BV4832.3 (ebook) | DDC 242/.34—dc23
LC record available at https://lccn.loc.gov/2019055226
LC ebook record available at https://lccn.loc.gov/2019055227

Contents

Introduction

When the days drew near for him to be taken up, he set his face to go to Jerusalem.

—Luke 9:51

A journey has a destination, a goal. At one point in the gospel, Jesus sets out resolutely on the road toward Jerusalem, preparing to do what he must to fulfill God's work of redemption. There will be healing and teaching along the way, but ultimately it will lead to the cross—and through the cross.

In fact, Jesus was in Jerusalem for the Passover feast, recalling God's mighty deeds at the time of the exodus. The feast commemorated how God delivered his people from the bondage of slavery in Egypt to freedom in the Promised Land. It was at this time of year that Jesus was crucified. It was at this time that his followers experienced a new kind of deliverance, a new "passing over" from death to life, a mighty act of God that changed their lives forever.

This journey to Jerusalem is a road to our own souls. It calls us to examine our lives, to look within, to appreciate the personal invitations and insights that God gives to each of us. It calls us to value our travelling companions and to serve our neighbors. It also demands that we not avert our eyes from the ways we need to change. It asks us to turn from what is destructive in our lives and welcome the gospel message of hope.

Travelling this road is, therefore, not easy work. And yet, it is a celebration. It is meant to be healing for our wounds and renewal for our minds. It is infused with God's compassion and guidance. It brings wisdom and growth.

As disciples, we are invited to accompany Jesus on this journey. What do we need to learn from him at this point in our lives? How is the Spirit leading us?

This book is meant to be a companion for personal prayer. You can use it as a private retreat. Find a comfortable place to pray. Light a candle. Read a reflection. Thoughts or questions from your own experience may arise. Bring them to God in a spiritual conversation. Then, take time to just listen. When you are ready, close your session with the Lord's Prayer or any other prayer you like.

Although coming from the Catholic tradition, these reflections, rooted in Scripture, can offer nourishment to all Christians. For those who observe the liturgical seasons, these reflections are especially apt for Lent. You can begin the Prelude during the week of Ash Wednesday. The six sections, each with seven reflections, can correspond to the weeks of Lent.

We are always on our spiritual journey. That journey signifies the way of discipleship and prepares us for what we cannot yet see. It is the road that leads to Jerusalem, in the footsteps of the one who went before us.

> *Then he said to them all, "If any want to become my followers, let them deny themselves and take up their cross daily and follow me. For those who want to save their life will lose it, and those who lose their life for my sake will save it." (Luke 9:23-24)*

PRELUDE

The Road

The disciple simply burns his boats and goes ahead. . . .
The disciple is dragged out of his relative security into a
life of absolute insecurity . . . out of the realm of the finite
. . . into the realm of infinite possibilities.

—Dietrich Bonhoeffer, *The Cost of Discipleship*

Purpose

> *As they were going along the road, someone said to him,*
> *"I will follow you wherever you go." And Jesus said to him,*
> *"Foxes have holes, and birds of the air have nests; but the*
> *Son of Man has nowhere to lay his head." To another he*
> *said, "Follow me." But he said, "Lord, first let me go and*
> *bury my father." But Jesus said to him, "Let the dead*
> *bury their own dead; but as for you, go and proclaim the*
> *kingdom of God." Another said, "I will follow you, Lord;*
> *but let me first say farewell to those at my home." Jesus*
> *said to him, "No one who puts a hand to the plow and*
> *looks back is fit for the kingdom of God." (Luke 9:57-62)*

The "journey" is such a rich image in human consciousness. It shows up frequently in the arts, in literature, and
in film. It may be the travels of Odysseus, Huck Finn,
Dorothy, or Frodo. Someone has to get from here to
there. But the journey is not just about "getting there."
It's about what we learn on the way.

In Luke's gospel, when Jesus determines to set out
for Jerusalem, he invites people along the way to follow
him. One person seems eager. *"I will follow you wherever
you go."* But this one is cautioned: *"Foxes have holes, and
birds of the air have nests; but the Son of Man has nowhere
to lay his head."* When we start out on a journey, we may
not appreciate the costs involved. We are looking for an
easy ride and cheap thrills. But this journey entails more.

There's a spiritual geography to navigate. Depth will be called out of us. Self-honesty will be demanded. Are we ready for the investment? Are we committed for the duration? Are we "all in?"

Another says, *"Lord, first let me go and bury my father."* In both the Jewish and pagan understanding at that time, burying a parent was the highest duty. How strange to hear the words: *"Let the dead bury their own dead. . . ."* This is inconceivable. But Jesus is speaking about the consequences of being spiritually dead. He's talking about the inner journey. He's saying: The importance and urgency of being on this journey with me surpasses anything else in your life. If you don't yet see that, you could be fulfilling obligations with no awareness, burying the dead when you are dead yourself.

Someone else simply wants to say goodbye to those at home. But that one is told: *"No one who puts a hand to the plow and looks back is fit for the kingdom of God."* It sounds so harsh. But what are we really looking back toward? To what lengths do we go in order to avoid that inner calling we sense? We must be ready to let go of what was—the familiar patterns we've gotten so used to, the things that comfort us and medicate us—if we want something new in our lives. Be open to finding something new, we're being told, something that addresses our deepest questions and highest hopes. That newness is what Jesus calls the kingdom of God. Everything pales when compared to it. And everything is enlivened when we seek it.

Prophetic words can seem harsh at times. But they are also practical. They speak to our core identity, our depths, and from there daily decisions and actions flow.

Perhaps you've seen or read some of the many books written by business gurus that promise to turn your company around. They deal with organizational structures, strategic planning, time management, and assessment. Or, think of the self-help tapes or podcasts that purport to improve your personal life and relationships. They all get very nitty-gritty and practical. But the best of them usually begin by addressing the question of purpose. One must ask: What is most important to me? What are my deepest values?

You must take another road to handle those questions. You must listen to your soul. Our soul, that deep life within us, created in the image of God, is not fed with superficiality, with illusion, with junk food. It's fed with authenticity. It's fed with truth, love, and service. Here, in the depth dimension of our lives, we are open to the movement of God's own Spirit. Motives are purified, goals are inspired, action is stirred. We remember who we are and consider what is most important in life.

How do we put our time and energy to work on a daily basis? Are we just managing the crises on our "to do" list, wasting energy on what is not very important to us? Or, are we listening to our souls? The smallest things can relate to our purpose: getting the kids to school, calling the friend we've lost touch with, attending to a customer, volunteering in the community, getting to church. All these can be ways of advancing our priorities and core values. All can be ways of choosing forgiveness, freedom, generosity, compassion. *"Let the dead bury their own dead. . . ."* This journey is all about life.

> *They said to each other, "Were not our hearts burning within us while he was talking to us on the road, while he was opening the scriptures to us?" (Luke 24:32)*

Roads run all through the Scriptures. Another source, the famous poem by Robert Frost, offers some grist as well:

> Two roads diverged in a wood, and I—
> I took the one less traveled by,
> And that has made all the difference.[1]

If we were to trace our path through life up till now, our impressions might vary greatly. Sometimes the road we travelled was wide and smooth, a superhighway. Other times, it was a rocky and narrow path, winding and treacherous. Sometimes it was well lit and easy to maneuver. Other times it was dark, and we couldn't see what lay ahead. Sometimes we had lots of company. Other times we felt alone.

On this road, may we discover the one who meets us wherever we are and calls us by name—the only one who can open the Scriptures for us and inflame our hearts, who brings food for the journey and enlightens the great road ahead of us.

(

ONE

The Desert

The beginner must look upon himself as making a garden, wherein our Lord may take His delight, but in a soil unfruitful and abounding in weeds.

—Teresa of Avila, *The Life*

Sin and Grace

In the fourth century, in Egypt, there were individuals known as the Desert Fathers and the Desert Mothers. These were people who left the cities and went out into the wilderness to live out their lives. Many of their sayings have been collected. In fact, one of the first Christian biographies was about one of them: St. Anthony of the Desert. People still read it.

These Desert Fathers and Mothers make it clear that they were not fleeing the evils of the city in order to find an easier way of life, an easier way to live their faith. They went to the desert to do battle. They saw themselves as spiritual warriors, going out to confront demons and to fight evil.

Where is the "battleground" for us? Ignatius of Loyola, in his "Spiritual Exercises," calls the devil "the enemy of our human nature." Going to the desert can mean going deeper within ourselves. There is a wilderness where we are tempted to turn away from our true identity, our true humanity.

> *And the Spirit immediately drove him out into the wilderness. He was in the wilderness forty days, tempted by Satan; and he was with the wild beasts; and the angels waited on him. (Mark 1:12-13)*

After being baptized in the Jordan River, Jesus must have felt ready for action. He must have been eager to begin his public work and teaching. But the first place the Spirit directs him to go is to the wilderness. The Spirit leads him to a forty-day retreat in the desert. There he is tempted in every way human beings are—by acquisition, power, ego, deception. He's tempted to live a less human life, to "sell out." He doesn't avoid that test. He confronts it and sees through it. He confronts the enemy and holds on to his humanity before God.

What will it mean for us to go to the desert? It obviously is not an easy course. It is not a tour through backcountry in an air-conditioned tour bus. This desert is not safe. There are dangers, beasts. But there is also the promise of truth, insight, and authentic growth.

I once heard someone use the term "lollipop theology." The person didn't have to define it. I could figure out what was being critiqued: a false, easy theology that avoids discomfort or doesn't "tell it like it is." It's a good point. It's not always clear, though, where the lollipops are lurking.

A preacher told me about a parishioner of his who approached him and asked, "Why don't we hear about sin more often?" Again, good point. A preacher who isn't dealing with the realities of both sin and grace needs some critiquing! However, the preacher had a feeling the parishioner was really asking, "Why can't you tell me: 'this is a sin'; 'that's a sin'; 'this can be a sin under certain circumstances' . . .?"

Moral theologians have a term for those questions: it's called "casuistry." There's certainly a time and place for that, for applying general principles to particular circumstances, as a help to guide our consciences. Yet, there's also a way in which relying on certain words and pat answers can be comforting, a lollipop, while the deeper call to a truer, more virtuous life goes unheeded.

Maybe we're not ready for that call. We'd rather have lollipops. If all you're interested in is whether "this" or "that" is a sin, you may not appreciate just how dangerous, how destructive, sin is. You may not understand the hold it can have on people, or how deep it runs. Capital "S" sin is a condition in humanity, a deep disruption. It's alienation, fear, deceit, illusion. It's a rejection of God's love and goodness; a rejection of what it means to be human. Getting at it requires going deeper than particular actions or inactions. It means looking beneath them. Actions can certainly be sinful; but, what deeper sinful attitudes underlie them?

> *Then the LORD God formed man from the dust of the ground, and breathed into his nostrils the breath of life; and the man became a living being. And the LORD God planted a garden in Eden, in the east; and there he put the man whom he had formed. Out of the ground the LORD God made to grow every tree that is pleasant to the sight and good for food, the tree of life also in the midst of the garden, and the tree of the knowledge of good and evil. . . .*
>
> *Now the serpent was more crafty than any other wild animal that the LORD God had made. He said to the woman, "Did God say, 'You shall not eat from any tree in*

> *the garden'?" The woman said to the serpent, "We may*
> *eat of the fruit of the trees in the garden; but God said,*
> *'You shall not eat of the fruit of the tree that is in the*
> *middle of the garden, nor shall you touch it, or you shall*
> *die.'" But the serpent said to the woman, "You will not*
> *die; for God knows that when you eat of it your eyes will*
> *be opened, and you will be like God, knowing good and*
> *evil." (Genesis 2:7-9, 3:1-5)*

It started with our first parents, as Genesis tells us, who were not satisfied with their own humanity. It wasn't enough to be loved by God as they were; they had to be gods, something other than what they were. Human beings chose illusion, falsehood, blame, attack, pride. And it has snowballed ever since, giving rise to actions and inactions on every scale: personal, social, and global. I like the assertion attributed to G. K. Chesterton that original sin is the only Christian doctrine that's announced in the newspapers every day.

The "desert" helps us to go deeper. When we turn off our distractions and start seeing things as they are, ourselves as we are, what will we find? One thing the Desert Mothers and Fathers found is something they called "acedia." It's a vice they defined as a kind of spiritual boredom or indifference, an aimlessness or coldness. They saw it at the root of so many destructive tendencies: lust for power, harmful busy-ness, isolation, cynicism, fear of vulnerability. Some pastoral theologians use the image of "warm sins" and "cold sins." Warm sins have to do with excess, and they say most people are obsessed with those. But it's the cold sins, they say, that should concern us more. They arise from acedia: from fear of passion, or a calculated apathy. They signal a dying soul.

If you are familiar with Dante's *Inferno*, you know that the poet's journey through the rings of hell finally brings him to the center point where Satan is encased in ice. A strange image? Saint Anthony of the Desert would probably find it fitting. Beneath the fires, the anger, hurting, blaming, and violence is that coldness that refuses to abandon itself to the love of God.

The road we're on invites us into the desert, the wilderness within, to do battle. It can be a time for coming to understand more deeply the destructive power of sin and the life-giving power of grace. We need to see how we've gotten into this mess, and how we can get out of it. What really changes people? Where's the power that liberates, heals, and saves?

We need to spend time with this, because that's where the gospel spends its time. That's why we call it "good news." It's a way out of sin. It answers our deepest questions and needs. It brings us to life.

Adam

So if we want to avoid that so-called "lollipop theology," we had better ask ourselves what being a faithful adult is like. How do we mature in faith? We might ask how we mature in any area of our life. We grow—physically, emotionally, relationally—in stages. Our psychosocial development occurs as we confront new experiences and our minds are stretched. On one level we must be ready for more growth, and then life provides events and tasks that demand it. Developmental theorists speak of "crises" that every individual must confront and negotiate as part of growing up. These include finding a sense of personal and group identity, searching for meaningful work, falling in love, and dealing with death.

Growth doesn't happen in a vacuum. It involves other people who accompany, challenge, or mentor us. Maturity involves relating to other people. The same can be said of spiritual development. It doesn't just happen in private prayer. There are personal and communal, private and public dimensions to our growth in faith. A church community provides places and events where we can express our beliefs and find support for our personal growth. We need that group identity. We need to know we have companions on the journey. Do we have someone with whom we can share our faith journey? Do we have models or mentors we can look up to and ask advice from?

Some churches have specific rites or sacraments related to this kind of personal sharing. Others experience this on retreats or in spiritual direction with friends or pastors. These can be great occasions for growth. But it isn't automatic. I heard a priest once refer to the confessional in his church (the place set aside for people to come and confess their sins and seek guidance) as a "time machine." He said it wasn't uncommon for an adult to walk into it and suddenly be back in the third grade!

When we try to evaluate our discipleship, or examine our conscience, and find that we are having the same experience as we did in the third grade, we're still on lollipops. We must allow the Spirit to stretch us, to help us grow in our spiritual lives as we do in every other area of life. Priests who celebrate the sacrament of reconciliation will often try to guide those who come to them to look below specific actions or omissions, to the attitudes and fears at their root. They may ask the penitent to deal with the question: "What is keeping me from being all the Lord is calling me to be?" That's about allowing the light to shine into the dark corners of our life, and claiming the power that God's grace offers us. That's the beginning of a new life.

> *Therefore, just as sin came into the world through one man, and death came through sin, and so death spread to all because all have sinned— sin was indeed in the world before the law, but sin is not reckoned when there is no law. Yet death exercised dominion from Adam to Moses, even over those whose sins were not like the transgression of Adam, who is a type of the one who was to come.*
>
> *But the free gift is not like the trespass. For if the many died through the one man's trespass, much more surely have the grace of God and the free gift in the grace of the one man, Jesus Christ, abounded for the many. And the*

> *free gift is not like the effect of the one man's sin. For the*
> *judgment following one trespass brought condemnation,*
> *but the free gift following many trespasses brings*
> *justification. If, because of the one man's trespass, death*
> *exercised dominion through that one, much more surely*
> *will those who receive the abundance of grace and the*
> *free gift of righteousness exercise dominion in life through*
> *the one man, Jesus Christ. (Romans 5:15-17)*

Saint Paul's letter to the Romans may be his most complex epistle. Yet its imagery can be both simple and profound. Here he refers to both Adam and Jesus as "types" (we might say "brands," or modes of being). Just as we are united in the first Adam, in our common humanity, in both our created goodness and our fallen nature, so we can be united in the new Adam, in a new way of being that transcends our old selves.

What is the way out of the disruption, the suffering, and the destructiveness that come from sin? What is the way to restoration, to healing, and to a fuller life? People do not change because they are given a law, or because they experience guilt, or because they have a lot of will power. We cannot muster an adequate response to sin on our power alone. Sin is a bigger problem, and it needs a bigger solution. We need a higher power.

People change through an experience. Experience is all encompassing. Experience shines through the spirit of the law. Experience is what the gospels testify to. It is an experience that recognizes the gracious love of God poured out in Christ, the new Adam, who entered our human condition, who went to those deepest, darkest places, into the disruption, illusion, and fear, into sin and death itself. He went there and shined a light. He brought God's love and mercy there, into that darkness.

How do things start to change? Through an encounter with Jesus—an experience that renews our minds, captures our imaginations, and reorders our lives.

Our spiritual maturity comes both personally and communally. We're in this together. We're united to Adam, sharing the same human nature, and to the new Adam, sharing the promise found in him. And so we go to the desert, not alone, but together. We go to pray together and to repent together. We go together to meet the Lord. That is the way of growth, of maturity.

> *Therefore just as one man's trespass led to condemnation for all, one man's act of righteousness leads to justification and life for all. For just as by the one man's disobedience the many were made sinners, so by the one man's obedience the many will be made righteous. (Romans 5:18-19)*

~

The First Desert

When you have come into the land that the LORD your God is giving you as an inheritance to possess, and you

possess it, and settle in it, you shall take some of the first
of all the fruit of the ground, which you harvest from the
land that the LORD your God is giving you, and you shall
put it in a basket and go to the place that the LORD your
God will choose as a dwelling for his name. You shall go
to the priest who is in office at that time, and say to him,
"Today I declare to the LORD your God that I have come
into the land that the LORD swore to our ancestors to give
us." When the priest takes the basket from your hand
and sets it down before the altar of the LORD your God,
you shall make this response before the LORD your God:
"A wandering Aramean was my ancestor; he went down
into Egypt and lived there as an alien, few in number,
and there he became a great nation, mighty and
populous. When the Egyptians treated us harshly and
afflicted us, by imposing hard labor on us, we cried to the
LORD, the God of our ancestors; the LORD heard our
voice and saw our affliction, our toil, and our oppression.
The LORD brought us out of Egypt with a mighty hand
and an outstretched arm, with a terrifying display of
power, and with signs and wonders; and he brought us
into this place and gave us this land, a land flowing with
milk and honey." (Deuteronomy 26:1-9)

Moses led the Israelites from the slavery of Egypt to the
Promised Land, the place where they would be free to
be themselves. Along the way he instructed them in the
laws and rituals that they would carry out once they got
there. But before they got there, they had to cross a

desert. The distance was not great, yet it took them forty years. It shouldn't have, but it did. What made the journey so hard? Why were there so many obstacles?

The people had been slaves for generations in Egypt. They had absorbed the messages of slavery. They thought of themselves as slaves, acted like slaves. They thought of themselves as having no worth. It's not easy to get to the Promised Land after all that. It's not easy to change your whole view of yourself. As much as we human beings wish we could get everything we want in a hurry, in an instant, there is much learning that has to happen first—and much unlearning.

The people of Israel had to pass through the desert to learn how to be free. They had to stop thinking of themselves as slaves—and start thinking and acting as free people. They had to realize what it means to be God's people, to have worth, to have dreams, to be loved.

People have to learn through experience how to be free. For the Israelites, that meant dealing with obstacles. It meant a lot of falling down and getting up again. There were times they wanted to quit, to go back to being slaves in Egypt. That was familiar territory. At least their masters gave them food. But this desert was too hard. It demanded too much from them.

They learned God's patience. They learned that when they were hungry, God would lead them to food. When they were thirsty, water would flow from the rocks. They learned to trust in the God of their liberation, the one who had sparked the idea of freedom in them and taught them to hope for a better life. This God believed in them. This God would guide them through the desert and make them ready to receive the promise.

Some never made it, though. In fact, most of the slave generation died off in the desert. But they died passing on the dream to their children. Even Moses only gets to the edge of the Promised Land. What a story our spiritual ancestors tell us from that desert!

Where's our Promised Land? Where's the treasure for us? What is truly valuable? Deep, deep within, what are you yearning for? Before you get there, you may have to wander through a desert. You may not be ready to receive it yet. You have to be prepared for it. You must learn some things first. Now, if you're like me, you probably don't want to hear that. But the message of this desert is: Trust. Someone is leading you.

> *"So now I bring the first of the fruit of the ground that you, O LORD, have given me." You shall set it down before the LORD your God and bow down before the LORD your God. (Deuteronomy 26:10)*

Moses gives the people a ritual that they must perform at the time of the harvest. We might normally think of harvest festivals as happy events. This is the time, Moses tells them, when you are to remember the desert. Remember all that your ancestors went through to bring you to this place. Remember the cost of your growth. When you think of where you've come from, it will challenge you to consider where you are going. Are you still moving towards freedom? There are always forces at work that want to pull you back into slavery. So, you must remember who you are and who God is for you.

Bring *"the first of all the fruit of the ground"* to God at this time, Moses tells them. Bring the best you have to offer, and put it before the altar of God. This is a recognition of the source of our gifts, a remembrance of the most valuable thing in our lives.

For us, a "desert experience" is an opportunity to look deeper into ourselves and ask: Are we still moving towards freedom? What slaveries, addictions or fears keep us from the Promised Land? What do we value most in our lives? Where is our treasure? Are we learning from our failures? Do we get up after we fall?

This is a time to remember our best and bring the "first fruits" to the altar of God; a time to remember what God has done for us, and to consider what God sees in us. It is time to let God prepare us for a new kind of freedom.

The Second Desert

Then Jesus was led up by the Spirit into the wilderness to be tempted by the devil. He fasted forty days and forty nights, and afterwards he was famished. The tempter came and said to him, "If you are the Son of God, command these stones to become loaves of bread." But he answered, "It is written,

> 'One does not live by bread alone,
> > but by every word that comes from the mouth
> > of God.'"

Then the devil took him to the holy city and placed him on the pinnacle of the temple, saying to him, "If you are the Son of God, throw yourself down; for it is written,

> 'He will command his angels concerning you,'
> > and 'On their hands they will bear you up,
> > so that you will not dash your foot against a stone.'"

Jesus said to him, "Again it is written, 'Do not put the Lord your God to the test.'"

Again, the devil took him to a very high mountain and showed him all the kingdoms of the world and their splendor; and he said to him, "All these I will give you, if you will fall down and worship me." Jesus said to him, "Away with you, Satan! for it is written,

> 'Worship the Lord your God,
> > and serve only him.'"

Then the devil left him, and suddenly angels came and waited on him. (Matthew 4:1-11)

There is another significant desert in the Scriptures. It is the desert the Messiah enters at the beginning of his ministry. Before he embarks on his public activity, he goes to a place—for forty days and forty nights—where he can be alone, where he can confront who he is and consider where he is going. He is *"led up by the Spirit"* to this place. Why? The Messiah recapitulates the story of the chosen people in his own life. Jesus learns from the story of his own people. He must struggle as they did—and pass through a desert to freedom.

> *For we do not have a high priest who is unable to sympathize with our weaknesses, but we have one who in every respect has been tested as we are, yet without sin. (Hebrews 4:15)*

The Messiah sums up the whole human story before God. He wants to experience it all: the deepest yearnings as well as the obstacles. He is tempted, as we are, to fall back when things get tough, to forfeit his identity, to compromise his goals. Yet, in each temptation he does not fall back. He stands firm in his identity, trusting God as his center. And he embodies a wisdom that beckons us to a new Promised Land.

First, there is a temptation to turn stones into bread. We are tempted to satisfy our hungers at any price, to reduce the meaning of our lives to our appetites. We pursue material things, power, or people in a way that makes them the basis of our lives. We believe that acquiring more and more things will save us.

Many people chase that path, and they become weak, fragmented people. They look to things to give what they cannot. They satisfy only a part of themselves, while the wholeness they desperately seek eludes them. The deepest parts of themselves are starving.

Are we going to learn from the Messiah? Will we be able to keep moving towards freedom? Can we say: Not bread (or any other good thing) alone, but God alone? God alone saves, and God alone satisfies the depth within us. It is God who teaches how all the rest can be received, enjoyed, used well, and shared.

Second, there is the temptation to throw oneself down from the temple, to test God's care for us. There is a temptation to manage our relationship to God based on our needs or achievements. Doesn't God owe us? Don't other people owe us? Haven't we done enough? Haven't we earned our positions, our titles? Don't we deserve more?

Many people are looking for that God or that other person who can be manipulated or coerced. They want to be flattered, obliged, and never challenged. They never get around to taking responsibility for their own lives. They demand. They test. They stagnate.

Will we keep moving towards freedom? The Messiah does not test, but trusts. Will we trust not in a title or position, but in the One who gives meaning to our life's work? God gives us what we need to deal with life on its own terms. God gives us guidance to make our way. God gives us strength to endure, power to serve.

Third, there is the temptation of *"all the kingdoms of the world in their splendor."* It is the temptation to displace our worship or devotion. What do we crave? Attention, a sense of importance, status, approval? Something will offer it to us. It may be a person, a group, an ideology, a drug. It may be our own ambitions. It will promise what we crave—if we make it the center of our life. We must give over all our loyalty to it; we must bow to its authority.

Many people do. They change themselves for it, betray their beliefs for it, sell out their friends for it. And then they experience the disorder and destructiveness that comes when their idols fall.

Will we follow the Messiah to freedom? Can we say with him: God alone will I worship? Can we say that nothing beside God will be God to me? That I serve the God of truth? And that that's where my inner authority, my liberation comes from? All else will flow from that.

We are still only at the beginning of this trek through the desert. There may be insights ahead that are meant just for you. There may be difficult thoughts or questions as well. We may face hunger or temptation. We have an example to follow. We can follow Jesus to our center, where God alone can provide what we hunger for. And we'll learn from him how to be more free.

∽

The Covenant

Then God said to Noah and to his sons with him, "As for me, I am establishing my covenant with you and your descendants after you, and with every living creature that is with you, the birds, the domestic animals, and every animal of the earth with you, as many as came out of the ark. I establish my covenant with you, that never again shall all flesh be cut off by the waters of a flood, and never again shall there be a flood to destroy the earth." God said, "This is the sign of the covenant that I make between me and you and every living creature that is with you, for all future generations: I have set my bow in the clouds, and it shall be a sign of the covenant between me and the earth. When I bring clouds over the earth and the bow is seen in the clouds, I will remember my covenant that is between me and you and every living creature of all flesh; and the waters shall never again become a flood to destroy all flesh." (Genesis 9:8-15)

We all know the story of Noah and the ark. Someone, a friend who was also an environmentalist, once pointed out to me something that I had never really appreciated before. It's something that is repeated several times in the short passage above: In verses 9 and 10: *"I am establishing my covenant with you and your descendants after you, and with every living creature that is with you."* Verse 12: *"This is the sign of the covenant that I make between me and you and every living creature that is with you."* Verse 15: *"I will remember my covenant that is between me and you and every living creature."*

What do you notice in those verses? With whom is the covenant—this solemn agreement, bond, relationship— made? How many times have we assumed the covenant is with Noah and his kin because God is addressing his words to them? But, actually, the covenant is with *all* the creatures of the earth, all creation. *"I have set my bow in the clouds, and it shall be a sign of the covenant between me and the earth."*

Another thing about this story: We often think of it as a children's story, probably because of all the animals, and the colorful images we see of the ark. But it's also a story about massive death and destruction. One parent I know mentioned to me how, when reading a picture book about Noah's ark with her children, they'd worry about the crowd of animals being left behind as the waters rose and the ark floated away. One picture showed an abandoned mother elephant wrapping her trunk around her baby. The kids were confused by all this pain. If the problem was human sin and wickedness, they'd ask, then why did the animals have to die, too?

It can lead us to wonder about the interdependence of all forms of life. It can lead us to ponder the interrelatedness of moral action, and of human responsibility toward our fellow creatures and the planet as a whole. There is a cosmic dimension to our faith, our decision-making, and our practices.

We may often think of the relationship of our beliefs to poverty, justice, social reform, and other human life issues. Have we often thought about the environmental aspects of believing in God's covenant with the earth? Yet the Scriptures and the church's teaching offer a rich foundation for reflection and action on behalf of a healthy environment that nourishes us and gives glory to God.

Christian teaching recognizes the solidarity of all creation. Humans could not exist without the animals that serve us, as well as all the living things that make up the web of life. There is a cosmic dimension to redemption as well, as St. Paul reminds us when he says: *We know that the whole creation has been groaning in labor pains until now (Romans 8:22).*

Yet, only humans are created in God's image, and so have a special role in relationship to the rest of creation. We can also reflect on how God uses the elements of the earth to speak to us. Sacramental churches use the gifts of creation as symbols expressing revealed truths: blessed water, palms, ashes, wheat, grapes, oil, incense, candles—all can carry visible meaning, and can express a response to God's word.

In the story of the ark, Noah turns out to be a partner with God, working to preserve life in all its diversity and interdependence. We're called to be good stewards, too, reflecting on God's covenant with all creatures, protecting God's handiwork, and honoring God in creation. The sign of the rainbow can remind us of all this.

> *For Christ also suffered for sins once for all, the righteous for the unrighteous, in order to bring you to God. He was put to death in the flesh, but made alive in the spirit, in which also he went and made a proclamation to the spirits in prison, who in former times did not obey, when God waited patiently in the days of Noah, during the building of the ark, in which a few, that is, eight persons, were saved through water. And baptism, which this*

prefigured, now saves you—not as a removal of dirt from the body, but as an appeal to God for a good conscience, through the resurrection of Jesus Christ, who has gone into heaven and is at the right hand of God, with angels, authorities, and powers made subject to him. (1 Peter 3:18-22)

So there is still more to this rainbow. Saint Peter brings up the story of Noah and the flood as a "prefiguring"—an image, a sign—of baptism, with the symbol of water making an ending of one thing, one kind of life, and bringing a beginning, a new kind of life. This is the ultimate meaning we find in God's plan for creation. In our created world, as in our bodies, we see the seeds of a new heaven and a new earth. Even now we can start living in that new creation. We are on a path of repentance and renewal. Clouds begin to part and a rainbow stirs us with hope and wonder. We are on the way to life, to a new awareness, to a new covenant.

~

New Wine

Then the disciples of John came to him, saying, "Why do we and the Pharisees fast often, but your disciples do not fast?" And Jesus said to them, "The wedding guests cannot mourn as long as the bridegroom is with them, can they?

> *The days will come when the bridegroom is taken away from them, and then they will fast. No one sews a piece of unshrunk cloth on an old cloak, for the patch pulls away from the cloak, and a worse tear is made. Neither is new wine put into old wineskins; otherwise, the skins burst, and the wine is spilled, and the skins are destroyed; but new wine is put into fresh wineskins, and so both are preserved." (Matthew 9:14-17)*

Teresa of Ávila is credited with saying to her sisters, "There is a time for penance and a time for partridge." In other words, there is a time for fasting and a time for feasting. Most Christians recognize fasting as a form of prayer that expresses our dependence on God and makes us sensitive to those in need. In some churches, Fridays are an especially suitable time for fasting and for remembering the meaning of Good Friday. We remember in a special way all that led Jesus to the cross. We remember the cost of our redemption.

We also remember that, as followers of Jesus, our fasting must be his kind of fasting. Jesus tells the disciples of John the Baptist that, unlike John, he is primarily a prophet of salvation. John's call was to preach repentance in anticipation of the coming of the Messiah. Jesus' call is to announce God's favor and the coming of God's kingdom in a unique way. He is the bridegroom who gathers people for the wedding banquet. Jesus literally spent his time uniting and reconciling people around food and drink. As a people of salvation we continue that never-ending celebration, imbibing the new wine of Christ's love and peace.

Jesus spent forty days in the desert fasting. He obviously saw the value in fasting. He says there is a time for that. There are times when we walk with the Lord through his fasting for our sake. We must see the cost, we must know the desert. But it is always his kind of fasting. It will always be his new wine that informs and gives meaning to our fasting.

> *Shout out, do not hold back!*
> *Lift up your voice like a trumpet!*
> *Announce to my people their rebellion,*
> *to the house of Jacob their sins.*
> *Yet day after day they seek me*
> *and delight to know my ways,*
> *as if they were a nation that practiced righteousness*
> *and did not forsake the ordinance of their God;*
> *they ask of me righteous judgments,*
> *they delight to draw near to God.*
> *"Why do we fast, but you do not see?*
> *Why humble ourselves, but you do not notice?"*
> *Look, you serve your own interest on your fast day,*
> *and oppress all your workers.*
> *Look, you fast only to quarrel and to fight*
> *and to strike with a wicked fist.*
> *Such fasting as you do today*
> *will not make your voice heard on high.*
> *Is such the fast that I choose,*
> *a day to humble oneself?*

Is it to bow down the head like a bulrush,
and to lie in sackcloth and ashes?
Will you call this a fast,
a day acceptable to the LORD?
Is not this the fast that I choose:
to loose the bonds of injustice,
to undo the thongs of the yoke,
to let the oppressed go free,
and to break every yoke?
Is it not to share your bread with the hungry,
and bring the homeless poor into your house;
when you see the naked, to cover them,
and not to hide yourself from your own kin?
Then your light shall break forth like the dawn,
and your healing shall spring up quickly;
your vindicator shall go before you,
the glory of the LORD shall be your rear guard.
Then you shall call, and the LORD will answer;
you shall cry for help, and he will say, Here I am.
If you remove the yoke from among you,
the pointing of the finger, the speaking of evil,
if you offer your food to the hungry
and satisfy the needs of the afflicted,
then your light shall rise in the darkness
and your gloom be like the noonday. (Isaiah 58:1-10)

The prophet Isaiah addressed those in his community who had lost touch with the meaning of their fasting and devotions. They were proud of their piety, and they didn't understand why God wasn't responding to them. "Look what we've done for you; why aren't you doing anything for us?" But God replies, "You call this a fast?" Instead of sackcloth and ashes, God sees their quarrelling, their fighting, their disregard for justice. God sees their hearts.

Traditions for tradition's sake, mere external acts of worship alone, do not impress God. These things must be joined to a sincere heart for true worship to happen. When that happens, *"your light shall rise."* The wine shall flow.

There is a Latin phrase: *Ars Una, Species Mille*. One Art, Many Forms. I suppose it refers to the one artistic impulse that underlies the many expressions found in all forms of art. We see that same truth revealed in different areas of life. One love is expressed in marriage, whether at the wedding feast, or in the tough times that require spouses to work through their issues. One devotion is expressed in our prayer lives, whether in the spontaneous and joyful moments of prayer, or in the discipline of praying when we may not "feel" like it, because we know its importance to our relationship with God. Love must underlie it all.

Fasting, as with all our spiritual practices or devotions, is a kind of art. What underlies it? There will be fasting and feasting at different times along the journey. But we will always be challenged to look again at our hearts, and to examine how sincere and open they are. Are we open to be embraced by the bridegroom who invites us to his banquet, to gather around his table? Are we turning outward, more aware of all those in need around us? Is the wine flowing?

Jonah

When the crowds were increasing, he began to say, "This generation is an evil generation; it asks for a sign, but no sign will be given to it except the sign of Jonah. For just as Jonah became a sign to the people of Nineveh, so the Son of Man will be to this generation. The queen of the South will rise at the judgment with the people of this generation and condemn them, because she came from the ends of the earth to listen to the wisdom of Solomon, and see, something greater than Solomon is here! The people of Nineveh will rise up at the judgment with this generation and condemn it, because they repented at the proclamation of Jonah, and see, something greater than Jonah is here!" (Luke 11:29-32)

Maybe it is part of human nature to "ask for a sign." Perhaps we've been in circumstances when we were tempted to pray for something, some "sign," that would bring instant clarity and erase all doubt. Maybe we were at the end of our rope, feeling so frustrated, and so we cried out in desperation. Maybe we knew what we should do in a certain situation, but didn't really want to, and so "waiting for a sign" became a convenient delaying tactic. Or perhaps we were in a situation where we realized that we needed help, that we couldn't face what was coming up alone, and so we humbly prayed for some kind of reassurance.

Earlier in the eleventh chapter of Luke, Jesus is confronted by opponents who condemn his ministry and demand a "sign." In the verses above, Jesus is addressing those who failed to recognize God's work in him, those who ask for a sign as a way to test God. He basically tells them: You've got your sign already. And he reminds them of the story of the prophet Jonah.

You probably remember some of the more colorful details of that story from the Old Testament. God directs the prophet to the pagan city of Nineveh to preach repentance, but Jonah doesn't want to go. He hates these ruthless enemies of Israel, and he goes to great lengths to avoid the call. God likewise goes to great lengths, to the point of sending a great fish to swallow him and spit him out where he needs to be!

> *The word of the LORD came to Jonah a second time, saying, "Get up, go to Nineveh, that great city, and proclaim to it the message that I tell you." So Jonah set out and went to Nineveh, according to the word of the LORD. Now Nineveh was an exceedingly large city, a three days' walk across. Jonah began to go into the city, going a day's walk. And he cried out, "Forty days more, and Nineveh shall be*

overthrown!" And the people of Nineveh believed God;
they proclaimed a fast, and everyone, great and small,
put on sackcloth. When the news reached the king of
Nineveh, he rose from his throne, removed his robe,
covered himself with sackcloth, and sat in ashes. Then he
had a proclamation made in Nineveh: "By the decree of
the king and his nobles: No human being or animal,
no herd or flock, shall taste anything. They shall not feed,
nor shall they drink water. Human beings and animals
shall be covered with sackcloth, and they shall cry mightily
to God. All shall turn from their evil ways and from the
violence that is in their hands. Who knows? God may
relent and change his mind; he may turn from his fierce
anger, so that we do not perish." When God saw what they
did, how they turned from their evil ways, God changed
his mind about the calamity that he had said he would
bring upon them; and he did not do it. (Jonah 3:1-10)

Jonah had a hard time understanding how God could
even care about these people of Nineveh. Yet somehow
his message actually got through to them. They heard
the word of God addressed to them, and they repented.
And there was nothing half-hearted about their response.
They became eager to change and follow a new path.
It's this reversal, this surprise, this example of faith that
Jesus holds up to his hearers—and to us—as a "sign."

Most of the time, like the people of Nineveh, we are
going about our everyday lives, not paying much attention to signs or the words of prophets. We experience

our typical frustrations, or we avoid doing the things we know we ought to. Other times we are hoping for more, humbly offering a prayer for help or reassurance. Will a sign come to us?

Well, what if the sign of Jonah is all around us? What if God is always sending signs? What if these signs of repentance and transformation actually got through to us, and we changed our ways? Lives changed by the love of Christ are the great signs that God gives to show us that he is alive and active in the world. People living according to the law of love in an age of selfishness, generous with their deeds of service, full-hearted in their response to suffering—these are the living signs, inviting others to hear, to listen, and to say "yes" to God's word to them.

On a desert journey, it's easy to become wearied or dissatisfied with our progress now and then. We may feel a little like Jonah, thinking that the possibilities of repentance or transformation are unrealistic. Then again, Jonah found God's grace moving in a place he least expected. It is a time for surprises. Even we can become the signs that God is sending to the world.

TWO

The Mountain

Faith is not being sure where you're going, but going anyway. A journey without maps.

—Frederick Buechner, *Beyond Words*

Sacrifice

*After these things God tested Abraham. He said to him,
"Abraham!" And he said, "Here I am." He said, "Take
your son, your only son Isaac, whom you love, and go to
the land of Moriah, and offer him there as a burnt
offering on one of the mountains that I shall show you."
So Abraham rose early in the morning, saddled his
donkey, and took two of his young men with him, and his
son Isaac; he cut the wood for the burnt offering, and set
out and went to the place in the distance that God had
shown him. On the third day Abraham looked up and
saw the place far away. Then Abraham said to his young
men, "Stay here with the donkey; the boy and I will go
over there; we will worship, and then we will come back
to you." Abraham took the wood of the burnt offering and
laid it on his son Isaac, and he himself carried the fire
and the knife. So the two of them walked on together.
Isaac said to his father Abraham, "Father!" And he said,
"Here I am, my son." He said, "The fire and the wood
are here, but where is the lamb for a burnt offering?"
Abraham said, "God himself will provide the lamb for
a burnt offering, my son." So the two of them walked on
together.*

*When they came to the place that God had shown
him, Abraham built an altar there and laid the wood in
order. He bound his son Isaac, and laid him on the altar,
on top of the wood. Then Abraham reached out his hand
and took the knife to kill his son. But the angel of the*

LORD called to him from heaven, and said, "Abraham,
Abraham!" And he said, "Here I am." He said, "Do not
lay your hand on the boy or do anything to him; for now
I know that you fear God, since you have not withheld
your son, your only son, from me." And Abraham looked
up and saw a ram, caught in a thicket by its horns.
Abraham went and took the ram and offered it up as a
burnt offering instead of his son. So Abraham called that
place "The LORD will provide"; as it is said to this day,
"On the mount of the LORD it shall be provided."
(Genesis 22:1-14)

There is no one who has a family, a spouse, a child, or a
true friend who does not know what it means to sacrifice. There's no one who has a desire, a hope, a goal—
whether professionally, artistically, or athletically—who
does not know what it means to sacrifice. No one who
has a passion, no one who loves, does not or will not
know what it means to sacrifice, to give oneself over to
a higher good, to lay oneself down in love.

We're all children of Abraham, and this story from
Genesis, as mysterious and strange to our ears as it is,
has something for us. There may be many levels to this
story, many ways to enter it. Consider these three.

The first level we could call the historical or social
level. A pastor told me once of a man in his parish who,
after hearing this reading proclaimed in church, came
to him upset. The man said that he and his wife had just
had a baby, a new son. "I can't tell you how much I love

him," he said. "And I can't understand a God who would demand a human being to sacrifice his child. I can't accept that." You can understand how the man could be so visibly shaken.

The pastor shared with him what scholars tell us about the time and setting of this story, how the people of Israel were surrounded by tribes that practiced human sacrifice to their gods, and how they may have felt pressure to do the same. On one level, this story is a teaching tool. It explained to God's people how they were different. It told them: Our God is not like these other gods. Our God does not demand human sacrifice.

With this context, it's easier to understand how, instead of representing some kind of flaw, this story was an opening to growth, an important step in the chosen people's understanding of God. But as interesting and helpful as this historical-critical level can be, it's not enough. We can go deeper.

A second level is a spiritual one. There are deeper theological or spiritual levels to consider in all of Scripture. The church has an expression for this: the *sensus plenior*, or the "fuller sense" we get when a passage is seen in the context of the whole story of the Bible.

There are great early Christian authors who see in this story a sign or figure of God's plan of salvation. Abraham's trust in God and love for God prefigures what we learn about God's love for us in the New Testament. When we reflect on this story, we'll see those connections, too. We'll see the love of the Trinity at work.

Abraham and Isaac journey together to the land of Moriah. The text says they gather wood, and that Abraham puts the wood on Isaac's shoulders as they climb the mountain. We can think of how Jesus put the wood of the cross on his shoulders and carried it to Golgotha.

Isaac doesn't understand at first what is happening. He says, "Where's the lamb for the sacrifice?" Abraham replies, "God will provide the lamb." Now, remember, Abraham was a very old man at this time, and Isaac was in the prime of his youth. At some point he must have figured out what was happening. As Abraham starts to bind his son, young Isaac could have resisted and broken away. He doesn't have to be sacrificed. He allows it to happen. Even though he doesn't fully understand, he sacrifices himself out of love for his father—just as Jesus accepts his role out of love for his Father. Jesus accepts his Father's will in love and trust. He lays down his life for his friends. In the wider context, the spiritual sense, we encounter the God who is so in love with us, so devoted, that he sacrifices it all for us.

In the story of Abraham and Isaac, an angel, God's messenger, mysteriously appears, reversing the story. In the same way, when Jesus' disciples come to the tomb in their grief and confusion, they hear an angel's voice telling them how God's power reverses the story of sin and evil. God's love triumphs over death and offers a new beginning.

That brings us to the third level. It brings us to ourselves, the personal level, where this story is about us.

We become the characters. We travel through the land of Moriah. This is the land where we must deal with our own confusion and grief. We come face-to-face with our need to let go, to sacrifice. We may not understand God's will fully, but we have to trust.

Consider this image: A woman was dealing with the death of a loved one and was having a really hard time with it. She was questioning life and questioning God. Someone told her to remember what it was like when she was a little girl and looked at pictures in a newspaper. If you put your face up really close to the paper, you could see that the print was composed of small dots that seemed random. It was only when you slowly pulled the paper away that the picture came into view.

We may not know how to connect all the dots of our lives. We're so close to them. They may not make any sense to us. They may be painful: the job situation that brings so much stress; the child who seems to reject our love; the illness that changes our plans. It's with God's perspective in our lives that we begin to trust. Things begin to fit together. It all becomes meaningful, good, and beautiful.

That's because we have a God who walks with us. Our God sacrificed for us to let us know that we are not alone in those experiences of life, to let us know that we are loved. That is what begins to transfigure our lives.

Pilgrimage

*Jesus took with him Peter and James and John, and
led them up a high mountain apart, by themselves.
(Mark 9:2)*

We often hear some Christian preachers or commentators
talking about how Christianity has nothing to do with
"religion." Or, we hear many others claim they are not
religious, but are "spiritual." Of course, all this depends
on how one defines religion or spirituality. When people
say "religion" they are often identifying it with corrupt
practices, or merely external observances, or distant
institutional structures. This, of course, contrasts with
true spiritual insight, prayer, and community.

These can be useful distinctions to make. They get
at the heart of true spirituality. Jesus, like all the
prophets, spent much time critiquing those who en-
gaged in religious practices in false, dishonest, or
superficial ways. He said, *"God is spirit, and those who
worship him must worship in spirit and truth" (John 4:24).*

Most people, though, use the word "religion" to
speak about human approaches to mystery, and the
communal practices that help guide people along a
spiritual path. Jesus participated in and honored the
religious heritage of Judaism. His parents brought him
to Jerusalem for the Jewish feasts. He continued to do
the same during his ministry. He celebrated the Passover
meal with his disciples, and in that context he gave them

the Eucharist, commanding them to celebrate this memorial of the new covenant that he was inaugurating in his own life's blood.

I remember hearing an interview with a rabbi in which he compared religion to fire. In the wrong hands, it can quickly get out of control and become harmful. However, used well, it brings warmth and light and is a source of civilization. Religious practices can be misused and abused—or they can be an expression of true spirituality and a wellspring for spiritual development.

The word "religion" can be broken down into its roots: *re* and *legio*. The meaning is to "link," or to "connect back." Christians are linked to Jesus and to his first disciples. We are linked to his inner circle, to Peter, John, and James. How do we express and deepen that connection through authentic prayer, study, and spiritual practices?

There is a saying from the east: "No one can create the light, but you can place yourself in the path of its beam." Our spiritual ancestors have handed on to us many traditions and practices that can help us wake from our sleep, appreciate the light, and feel its warmth.

One practice that is common to many religious traditions is the pilgrimage. A pilgrimage is a kind of walking or travelling prayer. It puts our prayer into action, into our bodies, over time. It reflects on life as a journey of spiritual discovery. Walking the medieval labyrinth or the traditional Lenten service known as the "Stations of the Cross," which traces Jesus' last steps, are examples of pilgrimage prayers.

Then there is the classic pilgrimage, an arduous journey, to a place of spiritual significance. You may have heard of the famous pilgrimage route in Spain known as the "Camino." It winds through northern Spain on the way to the cathedral shrine known as Santiago de Compostela. Tradition holds that St. James the Apostle, one of Jesus' inner circle, preached in the Iberian peninsula. He is the only apostle whose martyrdom is recorded in Scripture: he was beheaded by Herod in 44 AD, and his body was thrown to animals. It is said that the apostle's remains were transported from Jerusalem back to Spain in the ninth century. For a thousand years, the shrine that holds these remains has been a major pilgrimage site, and tens of thousands of pilgrims continue to travel there every year. They walk through the countryside, sometimes for months, to get there.

Emilio Estevez's film *The Way* portrays some of these modern pilgrims. Many have written about their experiences along the route. One account I read likened the experience to a lifetime in miniature: early optimism, midlife questioning, and later wisdom. It is a journey that yields its insights gradually over time, through aches, blisters, exhaustion, conversations with strangers, unpredictable weather, and new friendships. The pilgrims must receive comfort and must give support.

Dr. David Loxterkamp, a doctor from Maine, wrote of his feelings when reaching his destination in Compostela and descending to the sepulcher that holds the remains of St. James, the fisherman who knew Jesus personally and was personally called by him to share his message with others: "Here the span of two thousand years vanished instantly, and the living rejoiced with the dead. My heart seemed to ache with what God had uncovered inside me. Another miracle was worked: the faith of an aging, secularized American had become child-like again."[2]

There is a reason the church calls itself a "pilgrim people." We are constantly moving, constantly letting go, and constantly embracing what is next. Where are we on our own pilgrimage, our own journey of life? Youthful confidence? Mid-life focus or searching? Some other bend in the road?

Wherever we are, today we are linked. We're linked to Peter, John, and James, who had Jesus as their leader and companion as they climbed mountains. We're linked with one another as we gather around the eucharistic table in spirit and truth. We're linked with the Lord who chooses to walk with us down every road we take.

~

Altered States

Jesus took with him Peter and John and James, and went up on the mountain to pray. And while he was praying, the appearance of his face changed, and his clothes became dazzling white. Suddenly they saw two men, Moses and Elijah, talking to him. They appeared in glory and were speaking of his departure, which he was about to

*accomplish at Jerusalem. Now Peter and his companions
were weighed down with sleep; but since they had stayed
awake, they saw his glory and the two men who stood
with him. Just as they were leaving him, Peter said to
Jesus, "Master, it is good for us to be here; let us make
three dwellings, one for you, one for Moses, and one for
Elijah" —not knowing what he said. While he was
saying this, a cloud came and overshadowed them; and
they were terrified as they entered the cloud. Then from
the cloud came a voice that said, "This is my Son, my
Chosen; listen to him!" When the voice had spoken,
Jesus was found alone. And they kept silent and in
those days told no one any of the things they had seen.
(Luke 9:28-36)*

It's interesting, given that his gospel is not the earliest, that some scholars say that Luke preserves the earliest form of the transfiguration story. When it comes to stories like these, there are different approaches to interpreting them. At one end of the spectrum, there are those who seem to reduce everything to a literary device. At the other end, there are those who never want to examine or explore deeper levels of meaning in a text. They think everything must always be taken in the most literal sense.

For mainstream Christian traditions, however, this comes down to experience. The earliest disciples were interested in communicating the honest truth of their experience of Jesus. These three disciples, part of Jesus' inner circle, experienced something on this mountain with Jesus, something real, that went beyond their ordinary perception or understanding of things. We might call it a deeper state of reality.

Studies in psychological anthropology have pointed out that the vast majority of the world's cultures include altered states of consciousness as a normal part of human experience. They are comfortable with the idea that a wider or fuller reality can break through to us at certain times or places, bringing a clearer understanding of reality, necessary insights into life's questions, or helpful guidance in making decisions. Even with our own cultural biases, we're aware of how a piece of music, a work of art, an experience of nature, or a social event can deeply move us. They can produce changes in our consciousness, and they affect the way we interpret our lives.

Ordinary experiences in prayer and meditation can transport us. Extraordinary experiences, too, may be more common than we think, which is why spiritual discernment is such an important gift in the church. Normal, sane, healthy people have these experiences, although they don't talk about them much. When they do, they struggle to describe these moments when heaven and earth seem to meet.

How do you communicate an experience that goes beyond words? We can hear in the account of the transfiguration a grasping for words or images: light, cloud, terror, glory. Luke even says Peter speaks *"not knowing what he said."* And yet moments like these are the ones that become the most real to us. They are milestones on the journey of our lives, reference points that help us interpret our experience.

We probably have our own milestones, special times or experiences, that serve us in this way. Maybe it was a moment when everything seemed so clear, a time of special insight, an "aha" moment when we felt we truly understood who we are and where we're going. Perhaps we were captured by beauty or enthralled by something we were learning. Or we experienced the deep satisfaction of some accomplishment—or the joy of love.

Peter, John, and James glimpse something of the glory of Jesus on this mountain. They receive a graced insight into who he is, the fulfillment of God's promises. It was a learning that went beyond their own powers or capacities. We can understand Peter's disjointedness and his wanting to build those "dwellings." He wants to stay there, in that moment.

But life is not all mountaintop experiences or "aha" insights. Not for Peter, and not for us. Sometimes there are doubts, uncertainties, and fears to deal with. Sometimes we must make decisions when nothing seems clear at all. Sometimes we forget everything we've learned.

Coming down from the mountain is part of the journey as well. Saint Mark's account of the transfiguration adds these words:

> *As they were coming down the mountain, he ordered them to tell no one about what they had seen, until after the Son of Man had risen from the dead. So they kept the*

> *matter to themselves, questioning what this rising from the dead could mean. (Mark 9:9-10)*

Jesus is modeling something for the disciples here. Mount Tabor, the mountain of transfiguration, is only a stop along the road to Jerusalem. Jesus is following his path to another mountain, one called Golgotha, a place that will involve suffering and sacrifice. It, too, will be a revelation of glory, but not one the disciples will recognize at first. They will have to grapple with its meaning, with its promise of redemption. Somehow this is the path to a new life.

Jesus leads the way on a path that we all must walk. Sometimes he will lead us up mountains—to moments of deep clarity and awareness. Other times we will have to walk in trust, not knowing where we are going. That is when those moments of clarity come to our aid. They become our reference points, core memories that inform our decisions and give us courage to act. They remind us of what we've learned. They help us remain faithful to our deepest selves.

~

Moses and Elijah

> *Then Peter said to Jesus, "Lord, it is good for us to be here; if you wish, I will make three dwellings here, one for you, one for Moses, and one for Elijah." (Matthew 17:4)*

On one level, we can easily explain the significance of Jesus' appearing with Moses and Elijah in the transfiguration experience. It means that Jesus is the fulfillment of the Law and the Prophets. Moses represents the revelation of God through the giving of the Law at Mt. Sinai; Elijah represents the whole prophetic tradition of Israel.

But for those first Jewish disciples of Jesus, there are other levels to this experience. How did they come to understand what this experience really meant for them? What did seeing Jesus and Moses and Elijah together offer them, especially later, when they needed guidance in interpreting the meaning of Jesus' passion? What did it bring to their lives?

Moses came to people who were enslaved for generations. For generations they were told that they didn't count in the scheme of things. Their families, their lives had no value. They were worthless. All this creates a culture of subjugation. People believe what they are told about themselves.

Moses had a job ahead of him. He confronts that culture, those deep patterns of thought, and says: You are a people, God's people. Your lives matter. You must start thinking differently. Slowly, the people's memory of their own human dignity awakens. Imagine the chosen people beginning to open their eyes and to wonder if all this can really be true.

As we've already seen, it is when they entered the desert that the real learning began. That's where Moses receives the law. It's not merely a rule book. The law calls them to freedom, to a new relationship with God. The law says we are not slaves. We will think like free people, act like free people. We will treat one another justly. That's what allows them to strike out for the Promised Land, for a new way of life.

> *See, I have set before you today life and prosperity, death and adversity. If you obey the commandments of the Lord your God that I am commanding you today, by loving the Lord your God, walking in his ways, and observing his commandments, decrees, and ordinances, then you shall live and become numerous, and the Lord your God will bless you in the land that you are entering to possess. (Deuteronomy 30:15-16)*

The first disciples came to realize that this is what Jesus "fulfills." The law made them a people, brought them out of the desert, and called them to freedom. Jesus is the one who brings this whole process to fulfillment. He brings the law of the Spirit. He shows them the fullest meaning of the law, not written on stone but in their hearts. He shows them this not by writing anything down, but in his life, his teaching, and his sacrifice. He demonstrates just how much God loves us, and thus how much dignity we have as children of God.

Then there's Elijah.

The law brought the people through the desert. They started to understand and believe in themselves as God's people. They struck out on a new journey, developing their own culture, art, architecture, and commerce, just like other free peoples.

But, like all other people, there is a tendency to get lost, to lose our bearings. The people forgot what Moses told them about the source of their dignity. There were times when they wanted to be just like the other nations, even if it meant compromising their identity, their covenant with God. Sin, idolatry, injustice—all ways to flirt with another type of slavery. Elijah came at a time like that. He came when people were forsaking their freedom and identity. They were abandoning the law, the unique insights they were given, and regressing into fear.

> *When Ahab saw Elijah, Ahab said to him, "Is it you, you troubler of Israel?" He answered, "I have not troubled Israel; but you have, and your father's house, because you have forsaken the commandments of the* LORD *and followed the Baals.". . .*
>
> *Elijah then came near to all the people, and said, "How long will you go limping with two different opinions? If the* LORD *is God, follow him; but if Baal, then follow him." The people did not answer him a word. (1 Kings 18:17-18, 21)*

God chose Elijah to speak for him, to call his people back. The prophet tells them: Do not forget who you are, and what God has done for you. Don't throw away your freedom, the hopes and dreams that God awakened within you.

Prophets continued to come to call the people to authentic faith, to remind them that the Spirit of God will heal them and empower them to meet the challenges they face. They accompanied them through their struggles, promising that God will continue to do great things with them.

And those first followers of Jesus came to see that he is the fulfillment of that prophetic mission. They experienced him as the one who speaks, heals, and acts in the Spirit. Jesus brings the Spirit with him, the Spirit of God, the Spirit of wisdom and power. It is that Spirit who reminds us when we forget and heals us when we fall. The Spirit of Jesus enlightens us in our struggles and empowers us to meet new challenges. The Spirit keeps moving us towards freedom.

Like Peter, James, and John, and like all those first disciples, we may have our mountaintop experiences. There will be times when all the lights come on and a fuller reality seems to break through. Glory breaks through. But, like those disciples, the tests will come when we must go down the mountain to our daily lives and decisions.

In Matthew's account of the transfiguration, the disciples fall to the ground, overcome with fear.

> *But Jesus came and touched them, saying, "Get up and do not be afraid." (Matthew 17:7)*

When we must deal with our inevitable problems and personal struggles, it will be our turn to hold onto our freedom and identity. We will need to remember who we are and where our freedom comes from.

People can have all the external freedoms and choices in the world, yet still be slaves on the inside. We need the One who "fulfills the law" in our life. Jesus gives us an inner freedom that teaches us how to find what we are looking for. False prophets will offer false freedoms and securities. We need the One who "fulfills the prophets" in our life. Jesus offers insight into true human needs; he offers the wisdom and power of the Spirit. That is what will guide us down mountains, and through the valleys, until we reach our goal.

Gravity

They were on the road, going up to Jerusalem, and Jesus was walking ahead of them; they were amazed, and those who followed were afraid. He took the twelve aside again and began to tell them what was to happen to him, saying, "See, we are going up to Jerusalem, and the Son of Man will be handed over to the chief priests and the scribes, and they will condemn him to death; then they will hand him over to the Gentiles; they will mock him, and spit upon him, and flog him, and kill him; and after three days he will rise again."

James and John, the sons of Zebedee, came forward to him and said to him, "Teacher, we want you to do for us

> *whatever we ask of you." And he said to them, "What is it you want me to do for you?" And they said to him, "Grant us to sit, one at your right hand and one at your left, in your glory." But Jesus said to them, "You do not know what you are asking. Are you able to drink the cup that I drink, or be baptized with the baptism that I am baptized with?" They replied, "We are able." Then Jesus said to them, "The cup that I drink you will drink; and with the baptism with which I am baptized, you will be baptized; but to sit at my right hand or at my left is not mine to grant, but it is for those for whom it has been prepared." (Mark 10:32-40)*

Have you ever had this experience: You were trying to talk to someone about something that was serious, or sensitive, something that was important to you, but they, for whatever reason, were not listening and just kept on talking about themselves? How did you respond? I can imagine someone at that moment feeling let down or discouraged.

In Mark's gospel, this is the third time that Jesus conveys his thoughts to his disciples about where his mission is headed. They are on the road to Jerusalem, and he tells them that he will be rejected by the leaders and will have to suffer. He's letting them in on something immensely important, giving them a glimpse into his passion, inviting them into a great mystery.

And how do the disciples respond? Do they want to know more? Are they supportive of their friend? Are they humbled before the depth of what is unfolding in front of them? No, they're too caught up in themselves. Two of them respond by trying to secure their status in the kingdom. The others respond with indignation, showing that they are just as much engrossed in that self-serving agenda.

In fact, in Mark's gospel, this is the second time after the transfiguration that Jesus must confront his disciples' preoccupation with their status. In the previous chapter, he even uses a visual aid:

> *Then they came to Capernaum; and when he was in the house he asked them, "What were you arguing about on the way?" But they were silent, for on the way they had argued with one another who was the greatest. He sat down, called the twelve, and said to them, "Whoever wants to be first must be last of all and servant of all." Then he took a little child and put it among them; and taking it in his arms, he said to them, "Whoever welcomes one such child in my name welcomes me, and whoever welcomes me welcomes not me but the one who sent me." (Mark 9:33-37)*

We know how the world around us measures importance or "greatness." It's in the title you have, the salary you get, the power you wield. It's seen in how much stuff you own, or how many people you can boss around. It's your glamour quotient, or your media footprint.

Jesus has something different to say. Importance is in the smallness of a child. Greatness is about the authenticity of your service. That's all.

I had to undergo some physical therapy once, and the therapist gave me an image that stuck with me. She spoke about one's "center of gravity." If your center is off, then the way you stand, move, work, and exercise will suffer. There will be less alignment, more stress on joints, uneven development of muscle. It will lead to aches and pains—or worse. You're setting yourself up for trouble.

In the course of the therapy it became pretty easy to feel where I was holding my center of gravity and, when it was off, to correct it. I had to unlearn some bad habits. I had to pay attention to my posture or movements, notice when I was stressed, and then align myself again, finding that intuitive, inner balance.

In the passage above, Jesus helps the disciples with some spiritual therapy. Where's our center? We've learned the habits of the world we live in. From the school yard to the corporate office, people are arguing or worrying about their status. We're entangled in a negative form of competition in which we must attack, or blame, or bargain. Someone must be defeated for us to feel good about ourselves, or someone must be begged for approval. All this throws off our spiritual alignment.

When Jesus brings a child into their midst, he is inviting his disciples back to the center. He reminds them of their true identity, and he reminds them that true greatness is found in loving service. Are we too caught up only in ourselves and our agenda? We need realignment. Are we consumed with our status or our petty gripes? We must come back to our center.

We're on that road with Jesus to Jerusalem. We're being prepared for a deeper awareness of his passion. We're being confronted with a mystery that is unfolding around us. How will we respond?

∼

Breaking Cycles

Then I turned to the Lord God, to seek an answer by prayer and supplication with fasting and sackcloth and ashes. I prayed to the LORD my God and made confession, saying,

"Ah, Lord, great and awesome God, keeping covenant and steadfast love with those who love you and keep your commandments, we have sinned and done wrong, acted wickedly and rebelled, turning aside from your commandments and ordinances. . . .

Now therefore, O our God, listen to the prayer of your servant and to his supplication, and for your own sake, Lord, let your face shine upon your desolated sanctuary. Incline your ear, O my God, and hear. Open your eyes and look at our desolation and the city that bears your

> *name. We do not present our supplication before you on the ground of our righteousness, but on the ground of your great mercies. O Lord, hear; O Lord, forgive; O Lord, listen and act and do not delay! For your own sake, O my God, because your city and your people bear your name!" (Daniel 9:3-5, 17-19)*

We have already spoken about sin as more than mere isolated acts, but as the condition that underlies them. It is a disruption that has snowballed from our first parents onward, creating cycles of personal pain and social evils.

The book of Daniel is about a prophet who lived during the Babylonian exile. It was written down, however, centuries later to give comfort to the chosen people as they endured another persecution, this time under the Hellenistic occupations.

The Jews at this time would have noticed the same patterns being played out. And the same lessons needed to be applied to their current circumstances. The cycles of personal and communal sin are intertwined with pain and social calamity, but God, ever faithful to the covenant, is their hope.

Daniel, fulfilling one of the roles of a prophet, prays for the people before God, showing the communal aspect of repentance. He also points out the basis of their healing: *"We do not present our supplication before you on the ground of our righteousness, but on the ground of your great mercies."* The source of renewal is not found in their own power, but in something beyond themselves.

In our own short life spans we, too, can recognize cycles of pain and disruption. I knew someone who chose to live and study in India for a while. When he returned, he spoke of a term that is used there: the "pain body." We live from the "pain body" when we live out of the hurts, wounds, or bad experiences from our past. They determine how we perceive and react to others in the present. We experience betrayal and we respond to others with suspicion or blame. We nurture resentment and we lash out with revenge.

These patterns become well-worn, and we don't even notice how much they are harming us. We get caught in these cycles that keep us from seeing clearly and responding appropriately. Where is the power to break these cycles?

> *There is therefore now no condemnation for those who are in Christ Jesus. For the law of the Spirit of life in Christ Jesus has set you free from the law of sin and of death. For God has done what the law, weakened by the flesh, could not do: by sending his own Son in the likeness of sinful flesh, and to deal with sin, he condemned sin in the flesh, so that the just requirement of the law might be fulfilled in us, who walk not according to the flesh but according to the Spirit. (Romans 8:1-4)*

The Spirit brings awareness, understanding, forgiveness. Saint Paul speaks of the *"Spirit of life in Christ Jesus."* God's mercy takes flesh in order to break the power of sin and death. Jesus breaks the cycles of pain and resentment. He doesn't do this by covering them up. There are those who think positive thoughts are enough to overcome negativity. But the negativity only gets covered up for a while. It continues to steal away our energy. Jesus breaks the negative cycles by engaging them and transforming them. He enters our lives and frees our energy.

Consider the following examples. Someone who has carried resentment towards a parent is able to face it, acknowledge what was wrong, accept what was good, and finally let go with a spirit of understanding and forgiveness. Someone else confronts the rejection they experienced in the past, and in the knowledge of God's love grows to love himself or herself and to act in that love. Christ gives us new experiences to live from, experiences of healing and peace. We start living not out of a pain body, but from a transfigured body. We start living in the light.

> *"Be merciful, just as your Father is merciful.*
> *"Do not judge, and you will not be judged; do not condemn, and you will not be condemned. Forgive, and you will be forgiven; give, and it will be given to you. A good measure, pressed down, shaken together, running over, will be put into your lap; for the measure you give will be the measure you get back." (Luke 6:36-38)*

I once listened to a radio program in which people called in to talk about their problems. One caller was going on and on with complaints: "No one shows any interest in me; no one invites me anywhere; no one lifts a finger to help me. . . . " The radio "counselor" responded simply: "What you want from others—you better be willing to give it."

I wonder how many listeners of the program recognized the echo of the gospel in that advice: *"the measure you give will be the measure you get back."* Simple. But why then so difficult for us at times? Growth is not magic, nor is it instantaneous. It takes time because it is about becoming a certain kind of person. It's about becoming the person we want to be.

This is a time for breaking old habits, old cycles, and building new ones. Here's a place to begin: *"Be merciful, just as your Father is merciful."* We can't give what we haven't received. Where do we need mercy? Have we gone to the Father with that need? Have we really received what God wants to give us?

When we find ourselves living out of a pain body, we must begin a new cycle. We must take in the experiences that God gives us to remind us of his truth and love: the glory of his creation, the people we enjoy, the experience of forgiveness, our personal gifts, our friendship with Christ. And we must start giving what we would like to receive from others. Give service, encouragement, forgiveness, or leadership. Give love wherever it is needed, and notice how that love will return, *"pressed down, shaken together, running over."*

Dangerous

"When you are praying, do not heap up empty phrases as the Gentiles do; for they think that they will be heard because of their many words. Do not be like them, for your Father knows what you need before you ask him. "Pray then in this way:

Our Father in heaven,
> *hallowed be your name.*
> *Your kingdom come.*
> *Your will be done,*
> > *on earth as it is in heaven.*
> *Give us this day our daily bread.*
> *And forgive us our debts,*
> > *as we also have forgiven our debtors.*
> *And do not bring us to the time of trial,*
> > *but rescue us from the evil one.*

For if you forgive others their trespasses, your heavenly Father will also forgive you; but if you do not forgive others, neither will your Father forgive your trespasses. (Matthew 6:7-15)

Christians recognize the importance of prayer. Living in an active, fast-paced world, it's essential to ground our activity in prayer. Christian prayer is also distinctive in some ways. The person who has converted to Jesus, besides finding in him a model and teacher of prayer, experiences something of what he experienced in his relationship with God, his Father.

He tells his disciples not to be obsessed with *"many words."* Fixation on the outer form of prayer can express the "Gentile" desire to appease or manipulate the gods or external forces one fears. That is not the relationship with God that Jesus possesses. We have a Father who knows what we need before we ask. There is no need for manipulation or fear. The relationship being witnessed to is one of trust.

There is a priority, then, in our spirituality. There is, first of all, a recognition of who God is: *"Our Father in heaven, hallowed be your name."* We simply align ourselves with God and God's kingdom, God's way, God's path: *"Your kingdom come. Your will be done, on earth as it is in heaven."*

Maybe it's because we hear it so often—even from our own lips—that we are numbed to the powerful immediacy of this prayer Jesus taught his disciples. It calls forth a radical trust in God in the here and now. I once heard a Jesuit preacher ask: "What if we heard it like this: *Hallowed be your name*—NOW. *Your kingdom come*—NOW. *Your will be done*—NOW."

A minute of prayer like that, with full knowledge, with full presence, would be a dangerous thing. It would be giving over our whole day to God's will. It would be the axis around which the whole day revolves. The day would become prayer.

Jesus lived in this knowledge, this presence, this realization. We may feel that we glimpse it at times, but he was always there. If we were to let this prayer become a part of our life, we may enter into his life, his power here and now.

So, first, there is the simple and immediate recognition of and alignment with God, the source of our being. Then we can turn to ourselves. There is no denial of ourselves and our needs in the world. *"Give us this day our daily bread."* This, too, is distinctive. There are religious traditions that seek only a withdrawal from the world in prayer, a kind of self-enlightenment or absorption into the void. Christian spirituality lifts us from the world, gives us an experience of transcendence, in order to bring us back to the world to transform it.

So, if we experience God's merciful love in prayer, that mercy and love must overflow from us into the world. *"And forgive us our debts, as we also have forgiven our debtors."* When it comes to spiritual goods, if we try to hoard them, we lose them. Our hands must be open to receive and to give. And we freely give what we have freely received.

Forgiveness is often a hard process, and it's my lack of mercy that I often need forgiveness for. But, following Jesus, who forgave from the cross, means seeing the connection between prayer and action, prayer and a life lived with others in the world. It helps to remember that forgiveness is a decision, not a feeling. Feelings will follow. And as we choose to forgive, we come to see that forgiveness is actually a gift to ourselves. No one is left off the hook. Others may still have their need for accountability and may still have to experience the consequences of their actions. Yet we choose not to be burdened by others' choices. Others may choose to tie themselves in knots, but we will untie those knots and leave ourselves free.

"And do not bring us to the time of trial, but rescue us from the evil one." Prayer does not pretend to avoid the harsh realities of life. It does not shield us from trials, questions, or difficulties, spiritual or otherwise. It does give us sustenance through dry times. It does open up our awareness, inspire our creativity, and strengthen our resolve for doing good. As C. S. Lewis once said of prayer: "It doesn't change God, it changes me." The earliest Christians relished the spiritual protection they sensed—and the new spiritual power they received—in prayer.

Finally, another great distinction: As Christians, our prayer is untied to Christ's prayer, because it is made to God, through Christ, in the Holy Spirit. It shares, then, in the very love of Christ and the Father. Our prayer, whether alone or with the community, brings us into that most intimate, sublime relationship that is the Trinity. It brings us into the mystery of Jesus Christ.

THREE

The Well

Love, and he will draw near; love, and he will dwell within you. The Lord is at hand; have no anxiety. . . . Are you puzzled to know how it is that he will be with you if you love? God is love.

—Augustine, *Sermon 21*

Thirst

He left Judea and started back to Galilee. But he had to go through Samaria. So he came to a Samaritan city called Sychar, near the plot of ground that Jacob had given to his son Joseph. Jacob's well was there, and Jesus, tired out by his journey, was sitting by the well. It was about noon.

A Samaritan woman came to draw water, and Jesus said to her, "Give me a drink." (His disciples had gone to the city to buy food.) The Samaritan woman said to him, "How is it that you, a Jew, ask a drink of me, a woman of Samaria?" (Jews do not share things in common with Samaritans.) Jesus answered her, "If you knew the gift of God, and who it is that is saying to you, 'Give me a drink,' you would have asked him, and he would have given you living water." The woman said to him, "Sir, you have no bucket, and the well is deep. Where do you get that living water? Are you greater than our ancestor Jacob, who gave us the well, and with his sons and his flocks drank from it?" Jesus said to her, "Everyone who drinks of this water will be thirsty again, but those who drink of the water that I will give them will never be thirsty. The water that I will give will become in them a spring of water gushing up to eternal life." The woman said to him, "Sir, give me this water, so that I may never be thirsty or have to keep coming here to draw water."

Jesus said to her, "Go, call your husband, and come back." The woman answered him, "I have no husband."

Jesus said to her, "You are right in saying, 'I have no husband'; for you have had five husbands, and the one you have now is not your husband. What you have said is true!" The woman said to him, "Sir, I see that you are a prophet. Our ancestors worshiped on this mountain, but you say that the place where people must worship is in Jerusalem." Jesus said to her, "Woman, believe me, the hour is coming when you will worship the Father neither on this mountain nor in Jerusalem. You worship what you do not know; we worship what we know, for salvation is from the Jews. But the hour is coming, and is now here, when the true worshipers will worship the Father in spirit and truth, for the Father seeks such as these to worship him. God is spirit, and those who worship him must worship in spirit and truth." The woman said to him, "I know that Messiah is coming" (who is called Christ). "When he comes, he will proclaim all things to us." Jesus said to her, "I am he, the one who is speaking to you." (John 4:3-26)

The story of Jesus' encounter with the Samaritan woman at Jacob's well is, on one level, a simple one. Jesus starts a conversation with someone. But like all the stories in John's gospel, it works on different levels. It points to a deep thirst within us, and a deep source of healing.

We're told that the Jews of that time *do not share things in common with Samaritans.* In fact, Samaritans were looked down upon as being worse than pagans. This feud had gone back centuries, from the time of the exile of the northern tribes of Israel. Some of the Jews who remained during the Assyrian occupation, in the region of Samaria, intermarried and mingled their Jewish beliefs with pagan beliefs. They took on pagan customs and even pagan gods. They broke the first commandment of the Law. They defiled themselves.

The Samaritans were not allowed into the temple in Jerusalem, so they built their own in the north. When the Jews fought a war for independence, the Samaritans sided with the pagans against them. The Jews responded by destroying the Samaritan temple. Then a band of Samaritans stormed the Jerusalem temple, profaning it, scattering the bones of the dead in the sanctuary. In Jesus' day, it was a common occurrence for Samaritans to attack Jewish pilgrims travelling to and from Jerusalem. Among Jews, it was a terrible insult to call someone a Samaritan. You did not talk to them or accept anything from them. They were unclean, and if you handled anything of theirs, you became unclean.

What about this woman? In this society, it would not be customary for a man to converse with her in public, and certainly not about important things like theology. She could not study the holy books. At the synagogue she had to pray behind a screen apart from the men. She could only observe. Her opinions didn't matter.

And there's more. We're told that she comes to the well at noon. This is the wrong time of day to get water. In this desert community, it's too hot to go out at midday. The other women would have come in the early morning or evening to get their water. They would have brought their children, shared the community news, helped each other. But this woman is not included in the community. Perhaps the others are gossiping about her. Who is she with now? Perhaps that's why she must come out at midday, alone. She's an outcast even from her own people.

She's had five husbands. We don't know the circumstances, but we do know that in this society it was the man who divorced the woman. After these rejections, she's now living with someone. Has she been left destitute? Has she given up on community, on herself? Has she learned how to be tough, how to manipulate others, and how to protect herself? Has she learned to hide her true feelings? Does she have any self-respect? Does she have anything left?

When Jesus asks this woman for a drink, he is confronting all these levels: religious laws that condemn, social customs that oppress, personal defenses that keep people hidden. He is confronting the pain of exclusion, the fear of vulnerability, the thirst for healing.

Jesus did what came naturally to him: He saw a person with a thirst and reached out to that person. By simply beginning a conversation, he dealt with all the systems and structures that kept her bound. He threw down barriers and invited relationship. He saw through the pain and rejection that had hardened her—and offered acceptance. He listened to her spiritual questions and challenged her with new insights.

And he does this sitting by a well. He speaks about a "living water" that can meet her thirst in a way that surpasses the dreams she had given up on. He speaks of the well within, a spring that will never fail. The woman of Samaria allowed the walls she had lived with so long to fall. She allowed Jesus to see her as she truly was, to touch her on the level of her deepest thirsts. It's a simple encounter, but it's a spiritual breakthrough as well.

The church asks those preparing for baptism to meditate on this story. That's because it's their story, too. They need to see past layers of defenses and deception, to the thirst that is deep within them, a thirst that they may have avoided in the past or that they find hard to explain. It's a thirst for truth, for love. It's a thirst for salvation.

It's our story, too. God cares about our thirst and wants us to find water. The Lord is always ready to start a conversation with us. It's a conversation about things that matter, because we matter to God.

This is our story, on both ends of the conversation. How many simple encounters fill our days? How many thirsts, hopes, and needs do we see in the people around us? Jesus tells us, his disciples, that there's a spring of water welling up in us. His own spirit wants to come to us in our thirst and, in turn, flow from us to others who thirst.

The Tables

The Passover of the Jews was near, and Jesus went up to Jerusalem. In the temple he found people selling cattle, sheep, and doves, and the money changers seated at their tables. Making a whip of cords, he drove all of them out of the temple, both the sheep and the cattle. He also poured out the coins of the money changers and overturned their tables. He told those who were selling the doves, "Take these things out of here! Stop making my Father's house a marketplace!" His disciples remembered that it was written, "Zeal for your house will consume me." The Jews then said to him, "What sign can you show us for doing this?" Jesus answered them, "Destroy this temple, and in three days I will raise it up." The Jews then said, "This temple has been under construction for forty-six years, and will you raise it up in three days?" But he was speaking of the temple of his body. After he was raised from the dead, his disciples remembered that he had said this; and they believed the scripture and the word that Jesus had spoken. (John 2:13-22)

We all fly off the handle sometimes. Is that what happened when Jesus overturned the moneychangers' tables at the temple? I don't think so. It may have been a spontaneous action, or it may have been planned. That's something we don't know. But we can say that this was not a whim. This is a prophetic act and is deeply meaningful.

There is a verse from the prophet Zechariah in the Old Testament, the last verse of his book. It speaks of the messianic age when God completes all things:

> *And there shall no longer be traders in the house of the LORD of hosts on that day. (Zechariah 14:21)*

So Jesus shows that he is fulfilling the prophets' expectations of the Messiah.

There's more, though. Do you remember that old definition of a "prophet" that someone came up with? A prophet is one who "comforts the disturbed and disturbs the comfortable." We might ask: In the situation Jesus found himself in, who is comfortable? Who needs to be disturbed?

We know that the moneychangers converted unclean Roman coins into the temple coins, the shekels, which could then be used to buy sacrifices to perform religious duties. And they did this for a hefty fee. People made a lot of money on the deal.

So it's a situation where the temple elite prospered while the poor suffered. Ordinary folks who were trying to follow their religion (they were required to make sacrifices often) were struggling. They were hurting.

Remember the time when Jesus confronted the Pharisees regarding the Sabbath:

> *One sabbath he was going through the grainfields; and as they made their way his disciples began to pluck heads*

of grain. The Pharisees said to him, "Look, why are they doing what is not lawful on the sabbath?" And he said to them, "Have you never read what David did when he and his companions were hungry and in need of food? He entered the house of God, when Abiathar was high priest, and ate the bread of the Presence, which it is not lawful for any but the priests to eat, and he gave some to his companions." Then he said to them, "The sabbath was made for humankind, and not humankind for the sabbath; so the Son of Man is lord even of the sabbath."
(Mark 2:23-28)

Jesus reminds them that there is a way that we can get our practices, duties, or traditions backwards. Then we lose the point they are trying to make.

He says the same thing on that prophetic day at the temple. It's as if he's saying: "The temple is made for humankind, not humankind for the temple." The priests and elites were very comfortable with the temple system just as it was, while ordinary people who were trying to find God, were being marginalized and burdened. Jesus, the prophet, says: This is backwards; it's upside down. By overturning those tables, he's making the point: I'm here to turn things right side up again. That's what the Messiah does.

What about us? What are we getting backwards? What needs to be overturned in our lives? That's what Jesus will do if we let him. He's not about business as usual.

What's upside down? We need to examine the destructive patterns in our lives: the sin, the compulsions, the things that we know aren't good for us, but that we've gotten used to. Do we want to overturn those tables? Do we want more health of body, mind, spirit?

What's backwards? Is it the values that we've gotten from the world? The standards we take for granted? Someone gave me an image once: The world is a big department store. But in the middle of the night, someone sneaks in and changes all the prices on everything, so that the cheap things of little value now have huge price tags, while the good, quality merchandise now costs very little. In the morning, though, when the store opens, nobody seems to notice. Everyone believes the price tags. They're fighting to get the things that have little value but that cost a lot, while the truly valuable things, the things that are really worth something, are being passed over, left on the shelf. No one wants them.

It's a funny image, but it strikes close to home. Have we surrendered our ideas, our values, our standards to the wider culture? How do we view success? Have we bought into the materialism that disappoints, the lust that objectifies, the power struggles that wound? The Messiah will overturn the tables. He will put people first. He will highlight the genuineness of our service, the generosity of our spirits, the authenticity of our relationships.

How do we judge ourselves and our place in the world? Do we create insiders and outsiders as a way to gain prestige or to protect ourselves? The Messiah will overturn those tables. He will disturb our comfort zones, our false isolation, our tendency to exclude others or to ignore the rest of the world's problems. He will teach us that we are part of one another, that we are neighbors, sisters, brothers. He will turn things right side up.

Of course, people don't usually welcome the prophets. We like our tables set as they are, as we're used to them, even if they're upside down. In John's gospel, after the prophetic episode in the temple, people come up to Jesus and basically say to him: What gives you the right to do this? What gives you the right to challenge the power of the temple? What sign can you give? He responds: *"Destroy this temple, and in three days I will raise it up."* It's as if he's telling them: Do you think this is disturbing? Just wait. There is another prophetic act coming that will really overturn the tables.

Jesus points them to a sign they cannot yet understand. He points to the cross and resurrection, the real sign of God's power over sin, death, and evil. It is God's power to set things right. It is God's love transforming us, God's mercy giving us a new beginning—so we can live right side up.

The Temple

Or do you not know that your body is a temple of the Holy Spirit within you, which you have from God, and that you are not your own? For you were bought with a price; therefore glorify God in your body. (1 Corinthians 6:19-20)

When Jesus spoke to those he upset when he overturned the tables at the temple, he said: *"Destroy this temple, and in three days I will raise it up" (John 2:19).* He was speaking, we are told, of his own body. Now St. Paul can speak to all believers using the same image: The Spirit of God is within them. They are temples.

In fact, the temple structure is there to remind us that God chooses to reside with his people. Religious obligations, rites, and traditions do not take precedence over people. They are there to serve people. When things take precedence over people, we are to remind ourselves that people take precedence over things.

How do we honor God's temple? A church building receives care and honor, it is maintained in reverence and adorned with beauty, because it recalls how God abides here with his people. Our minds are lifted to heaven so that we can see more clearly how heaven interacts with us on earth. The church is a place where we are fed by a community so that we can build community all around us, and so that we can serve our closest neighbor. It is a gathering place where we are refreshed in spirit, so that we can bring spirit to others.

How do we desecrate God's temple? When we treat others dismissively, we dishonor both the creature and the Creator. When we treat others with arrogance, judgment, hatred, or abuse, we violate God's handiwork. When we fail to object to the neglect, mistreatment, or exploitation of any person or human community, we fail to honor the dignity of all human life.

The way we treat ourselves and our own bodies is also an indicator of reverence for God's temple. Do we care about our health and what we let into our bodies? Do we give ourselves the rest and exercise we need? Do we give ourselves permission to de-stress from work and enjoy time with family and friends without guilt? Do we allow ourselves the freedom to adorn our bodies and to enjoy the good things of life? Are these not also ways to honor the Creator?

Rev. Thomas Ryan, in his book *Reclaiming the Body in Christian Spirituality*, makes the point that "the spiritual journey goes through the body."[3] He stresses that the spiritual life is not a disembodied life but rather a *life* in the Spirit. It is holistic. Christian theology has the highest regard for the human body. The incarnation, the resurrection, the understanding of the church as the Body of Christ, and so on—all these doctrines raise up the sacredness of our embodied experience. And yet Christian spiritual practice does not always display such high estimation of the body. Are we comfortable, are we free, in using our "body language" in prayer and worship?

> *One of the Pharisees asked Jesus to eat with him, and he went into the Pharisee's house and took his place at the*

table. And a woman in the city, who was a sinner,
having learned that he was eating in the Pharisee's house,
brought an alabaster jar of ointment. She stood behind
him at his feet, weeping, and began to bathe his feet
with her tears and to dry them with her hair. Then she
continued kissing his feet and anointing them with the
ointment. Now when the Pharisee who had invited him
saw it, he said to himself, "If this man were a prophet,
he would have known who and what kind of woman this
is who is touching him—that she is a sinner." Jesus spoke
up and said to him, "Simon, I have something to say to
you." "Teacher," he replied, "Speak." "A certain creditor
had two debtors; one owed five hundred denarii, and
the other fifty. When they could not pay, he canceled the
debts for both of them. Now which of them will love him
more?" Simon answered, "I suppose the one for whom
he canceled the greater debt." And Jesus said to him,
"You have judged rightly." Then turning toward the
woman, he said to Simon, "Do you see this woman?
I entered your house; you gave me no water for my feet,
but she has bathed my feet with her tears and dried them
with her hair. You gave me no kiss, but from the time
I came in she has not stopped kissing my feet. You did not
anoint my head with oil, but she has anointed my feet
with ointment. Therefore, I tell you, her sins, which were
many, have been forgiven; hence she has shown great
love. But the one to whom little is forgiven, loves little."
Then he said to her, "Your sins are forgiven." But those
who were at the table with him began to say among

themselves, "Who is this who even forgives sins?"
And he said to the woman, "Your faith has saved you;
go in peace." (Luke 7:36-50)

We may wish to sidestep the sensuality in this penitent woman's physical displays toward Jesus in Simon's home. But these are what Jesus calls the showing of "*great love.*" Her body language communicates her freedom and joy in encountering God's mercy. Here is an experience of the presence of Christ, the temple of God, and she must respond with her whole self.

In his book, Ryan speaks of a time when, in meditation on this passage, he felt called to enter the story physically and enacted his own penitential prayer. This allowed him to enter the meditation on God's word more deeply, more holistically. This became a key prayer memory in his life. He felt washed, purified. "I remained for a long time on the floor, filled with the kind of deep gratitude that is ready to give its life in return," he writes. "The posture of the body opened the door for what was in the heart and bid it come forth."[4]

There are many examples of the body language of prayer in the various Christian churches and in all religions. Standing, kneeling, prostration, the raising of hands, or dancing can all outwardly express the heart of the temple. Simple actions like making the sign of the cross, lighting candles, sprinkling water, or anointing someone with oil extend prayer into symbol and touch. They are authentic to the extent they show "*great love.*"

We are embodied spirits. We are enspirited bodies. We are temples. Reverencing the sacredness of ourselves, honoring our wholeness, leads to reverencing others and serving the world. It is prayer. It is honoring the Lord who abides within.

~

Images

At that very time there were some present who told him about the Galileans whose blood Pilate had mingled with their sacrifices. He asked them, "Do you think that because these Galileans suffered in this way they were worse sinners than all other Galileans? No, I tell you; but unless you repent, you will all perish as they did. Or those eighteen who were killed when the tower of Siloam fell on them—do you think that they were worse offenders than all the others living in Jerusalem? No, I tell you; but unless you repent, you will all perish just as they did."

Then he told this parable: "A man had a fig tree planted in his vineyard; and he came looking for fruit on it and found none. So he said to the gardener, 'See here! For three years I have come looking for fruit on this fig tree, and still I find none. Cut it down! Why should it be wasting the soil?' He replied, 'Sir, let it alone for one more year, until I dig around it and put manure on it. If it bears fruit next year, well and good; but if not, you can cut it down.'" (Luke 13:1-9)

Sometimes, spiritual directors or pastors use the term "image of God." They ask you to examine your "image of God." When they use that term in this context, they're not talking about a picture. They're talking about ways of thinking about God that affect our relationship with God. Our ideas, images, and patterns of thought affect us in many ways, for better or worse.

For some, religion is merely about self-esteem. It's there to help you feel good about yourself and the world. God is like a cosmic teddy bear, a new-age accessory that fits into our life and helps us blend into our world. God affirms, but rarely challenges.

For others, the message of their religion is all about guilt, terror, or the threat of hell. That's their motivation to stay on the right path. The way they relate to God may be no different than the way they related to authority figures as a child. I once heard someone say that when he thinks of God he hears his mother's voice telling him what to do—or not to do. He said, "I'm good when I think she's looking, and then when she's not I do what I want anyway." For many, their image of God makes them want to hide from God, bargain with God, or try to fool God. God is the enforcer, the one who's watching us, waiting to get us when we mess up.

Are our images of God in tune with Jesus' images of God? How do we see God? How do we hear God? In the passage above we hear twice: *"unless you repent, you will all perish."* How do we hear this? How do we put it together with what we preach about God's unconditional love?

The word "repent" relates to the Greek word *metanoia*. *Metanoia* is about conversion, about "turning around." When we look only in one direction, our view is truncated. When we turn, we get a whole new view. When we are free to look around, to see things from one side and then another, our perspective is more complete. We can see where we need to go. We can move in the right direction.

"Repentance," then, calls us to change, to growth. It calls us to be open to conversion, to a new perspective. As the Spirit leads, we can be open to new images of God. That's because there is always more to God. God will surprise us again and again, because as we grow, the Lord teaches us new things. Scripture, prayer, discipleship, new experiences—all these help us to grow. If we refuse to grow, if we choose to hold on to old images that have nothing to do with Jesus' images, then we may *"perish."* We may "waste the soil." We may die fruitless.

> *Moses was keeping the flock of his father-in-law Jethro, the priest of Midian; he led his flock beyond the wilderness, and came to Horeb, the mountain of God. There the angel of the LORD appeared to him in a flame of fire out of a bush; he looked, and the bush was blazing, yet it was not consumed. Then Moses said, "I must turn aside and look at this great sight, and see why the bush is not burned up." When the LORD saw that he had turned aside to see, God called to him out of the bush, "Moses, Moses!" And he said, "Here I am." Then he said, "Come no closer!*

Remove the sandals from your feet, for the place on
which you are standing is holy ground." He said further,
"I am the God of your father, the God of Abraham, the
God of Isaac, and the God of Jacob." And Moses hid his
face, for he was afraid to look at God.

Then the LORD *said, "I have observed the misery of*
my people who are in Egypt; I have heard their cry on
account of their taskmasters. Indeed, I know their
sufferings, and I have come down to deliver them from the
Egyptians, and to bring them up out of that land to a
good and broad land, a land flowing with milk and
honey. . . . So come, I will send you to Pharaoh to bring
my people, the Israelites, out of Egypt." But Moses said to
God, "Who am I that I should go to Pharaoh, and bring
the Israelites out of Egypt?" He said, "I will be with you;
and this shall be the sign for you that it is I who sent you:
when you have brought the people out of Egypt, you shall
worship God on this mountain."

But Moses said to God, "If I come to the Israelites and
say to them, 'The God of your ancestors has sent me to
you,' and they ask me, 'What is his name?' what shall
I say to them?" God said to Moses, "I AM WHO I AM.*"*
He said further, "Thus you shall say to the Israelites,
'I AM *has sent me to you.'" (Exodus 3:1-8, 10-14)*

I've heard that the name of God in this important passage is not easy to translate. Variations include "I am
what you need" and "I am for you." The Hebrew letters
for God's name, Y + H + W + H, evoke for some the

sound of one's breath. God is the source of our life. From our first breath to our last, God is breathing life into us.

"*I AM WHO I AM.*" God is Being with a capital "B." We are beings, but God is Being. Thomas Aquinas, the great medieval theologian, stated that God's Being, God's Love, and God's Truth coincide. It is all one. What would it be like for our being to be in step with, in harmony with, God's Being? What is it like to be in harmony with the Love that is at the heart of the universe?

We know what it is like to dance. Sometimes we may feel out of step, out of tune with the music. Especially when first learning a dance, we may have to look at our feet and think about the movement and rhythm. But as we learn, as we begin to resonate with the movement and the music, we let go and start enjoying it. We are living in harmony. We become the dance. What a wonderful image.

There was a great biblical theologian and ecumenist of the twentieth century named Augustin Bea. He was also named a cardinal by Pope John XXIII. He told a story of a time he visited an elderly lady, a shut-in, in her home. He noticed on the wall a picture of Jesus, one of those where it seems like his eyes are following you around. The cardinal commented on it: "Do you think of God that way? Watching your every move, keeping his eyes on you so that you don't make a mistake?" The lady gave him a confused look, and then replied, "No, it reminds me that God is so in love with me that he can't keep his eyes off me!"

It seems that Cardinal Bea was expecting to find a person with one image of God, but she showed him another. She was in tune with an image of God from the New Testament: Jesus as the beloved, the bridegroom, who can't keep his eyes off us.

Deep down we know what it is like for our being to be in tune with God's Being. That's our true self. But obstacles, fears, and false images get in our way. And we get used to being out of tune. It's time to listen, to clear away the obstacles, to "repent." Then, instead of withering on the vine, we will be alive, and we will bear fruit.

I can imagine the gardener in Jesus' parable returning to the fig tree every day to look for the buds that signal new life. As we nurture a right relationship with our creator, as we go to our hearts with Jesus, the bridegroom, we start blossoming, unfolding. We become more alive; our being is more available. We start sharing with others, caring about them, showing love. We start breathing. We start dancing.

∼

Forgive

Then Peter came and said to him, "Lord, if another member of the church sins against me, how often should I forgive? As many as seven times?" Jesus said to him, "Not seven times, but, I tell you, seventy-seven times." (Matthew 18:21-22)

I imagine Peter thought he was being generous when he asked if he had to forgive seven times. After all, the number seven signifies fullness or completeness in the Bible. Peter may have been looking for a pat on the back for being so bighearted, such a good student. But Jesus uses Peter's question as an opportunity to go beyond our human ideas about what is "enough." He exaggerates the numbers. He's saying numbers and measurement don't even figure into this question.

> *Lamech said to his wives:*
> *"Adah and Zillah, hear my voice;*
>   *you wives of Lamech, listen to what I say:*
> *I have killed a man for wounding me,*
>   *a young man for striking me.*
> *If Cain is avenged sevenfold,*
>   *truly Lamech seventy-sevenfold." (Genesis 4:23-24)*

In the earliest chapters of Genesis, we hear about Cain, who killed his brother Abel. Lemech is a descendant of Cain who kills two people. He shows how once resentment, violence, and sin are unleashed in the world their effects keep proliferating. There's no stopping this downward cycle until the whole world is falling.

That's the human story. But now, Jesus says, there is a way to undo that story. The cycles of sin can be checked. The measuring can end. We don't just have to cope with evil; we can overcome it. There's a new story here, and it's called the kingdom of God. God's story surpasses anything sin can do. It's the path of forgiveness, the power to bring victory to any broken situation.

Jesus was someone totally attuned to the human condition. He certainly understood how people could find it hard to forgive. But he does not compromise when it comes to the call to mercy. We can't talk about God's mercy while withholding our mercy from others.

> *"For this reason the kingdom of heaven may be compared to a king who wished to settle accounts with his slaves. When he began the reckoning, one who owed him ten thousand talents was brought to him; and, as he could not pay, his lord ordered him to be sold, together with his wife and children and all his possessions, and payment to be made. So the slave fell on his knees before him, saying, 'Have patience with me, and I will pay you everything.' And out of pity for him, the lord of that slave released him and forgave him the debt. But that same slave, as he went out, came upon one of his fellow slaves who owed him a hundred denarii; and seizing him by the throat, he said, 'Pay what you owe.' Then his fellow slave fell down and pleaded with him, 'Have patience with me, and I will pay you.' But he refused; then he went and threw him into prison until he would pay the debt. When his fellow slaves saw what had happened, they were greatly distressed, and they went and reported to their lord all that had taken place. Then his lord summoned him and said to him, 'You wicked slave! I forgave you all that debt because you pleaded with me. Should you not have had*

mercy on your fellow slave, as I had mercy on you?'
And in anger his lord handed him over to be tortured
until he would pay his entire debt. So my heavenly Father
will also do to every one of you, if you do not forgive your
brother or sister from your heart." (Matthew 18:23-35)

Jesus follows his call to unlimited forgiveness with this parable. It's not a pleasant one. It involves slaves and torturers. He takes a situation from the world of that time to illustrate how we can all be slaves to sin. And he shows us the way out of that slavery.

Ten thousand talents was a vast amount to owe someone. It represented twenty years of wages for the common person. When the king sees this poor slave begging for time to pay it back, he knows that he will never be able to do so. With his whole lifetime he could never repay. So out of "pity" the king simply forgives the debt. He throws out all the measurements of what he owes. In essence, he gives the man his life back.

And yet here is the tragedy. This man who has just been given a new life doesn't realize it. He doesn't appreciate what has just happened to him. We see that in the way he treats his peer who owes him a tiny amount in comparison to what he had owed. He is still under the control of his measured mentality. He is still living in a world of resentment, conditions, and payback. He is still a slave.

We're all in that same position. The message to us is: God has given us our lives back. We were lost in the story of human sin, because we're all part of it, and God did not measure the cost to ransom us. God poured out his own life to give us a chance. God forgave us and showed us a new way. If we come to realize this, if we can appreciate what God has done for us, if we really let it sink in—we'd be free. We'd be freed from our measured morality, our conditional love, our petty grudges. We wouldn't need them anymore. Life would look so different. Life would be such a gift.

And we would forgive. We'd forgive ourselves and forgive others. We'd see things as they truly are. We'd see others' pain and lack of awareness. Forgiveness is not excusing others for their wrongs or letting them off the hook in their need to grow. That's their path, not ours. But others will not have power over us. Forgiveness releases us; it is a gift to ourselves. Forgiveness is not a mere "feeling." It is a decision and a process. Feelings will follow as we remind ourselves of our decision to forgive.

Jesus calls us to the process of forgiveness because it is the way out of the pain and distortion that binds so many. He knew he could call us to this because of God's merciful relationship to us. As we live in that relationship, as we absorb it, realize it, let it sink in—we'll start telling a whole new story.

Discernment

*Now he was casting out a demon that was mute; when
the demon had gone out, the one who had been mute
spoke, and the crowds were amazed. But some of them
said, "He casts out demons by Beelzebul, the ruler of the
demons." Others, to test him, kept demanding from him
a sign from heaven. But he knew what they were thinking
and said to them, "Every kingdom divided against itself
becomes a desert, and house falls on house. If Satan
also is divided against himself, how will his kingdom
stand?—for you say that I cast out the demons by
Beelzebul. Now if I cast out the demons by Beelzebul,
by whom do your exorcists cast them out? Therefore they
will be your judges. But if it is by the finger of God that
I cast out the demons, then the kingdom of God has come
to you." (Luke 11:14-20)*

There is a spiritual gift known as "discernment." This
is not about having discerning tastes in clothing or food.
It's not about being a perceptive shopper. It's about
perceiving the underlying source of some activity or
influence. As we try to negotiate our decisions and
choices in life, we can be blinded by pride, perplexed
by the noise of the world around us. The "discernment
of spirits" is a charism, a gift of the Spirit, that helps us
make our way to our true goal in life.

People can be influenced by many things in this
world. We are influenced by our own depth. We are

spiritual creatures, made in the image of God; but we are finite, easily frustrated and confused by our drives. We must discern our path through our own human weaknesses and faults, our hopes and aspirations. We must learn to be true to our deepest selves that are yearning for God. We must be able to discern what bubbles up from our own humanity.

In addition, we must be able to discern where and how God is leading us in life. God is the source of the path that leads to life. The road might get rocky, but if it is leading to more truth, more joy in our lives, we can discern God's presence. If something is leading us to truth, to wholeness, to peace, God is there. Someone gave me a good principle of discernment once: The voice of God in your life will always be the voice of encouragement. Where in our experience do we find the encouragement to walk more closely with the God of life?

But there are other influences. Evil is inhuman. It brings disorder to our lives. It frustrates our plans. It makes right seem wrong and wrong seem right. It tells us lies about ourselves. It sends a message of discouragement.

The great medieval theologians called evil a "privation," a lack of some good that should be present. In other words, evil is nothingness, a void. But we empower it with our fear. We give in to its influence and turn away from truth. We see ourselves as less than we are—or more than we are. We pretend to be something we're not. We start living in the lies.

There are those who tried to distort Jesus' teaching and work. They lack discernment. They don't perceive the light he is shining in the darkness. They don't recognize the healing and freedom he brings to others as the work of God. And so they miss out. They don't see that the kingdom of God has come to them to heal them. They miss out on the joy he came to bring.

> *But this command I gave them, "Obey my voice, and I will be your God, and you shall be my people; and walk only in the way that I command you, so that it may be well with you." Yet they did not obey or incline their ear, but, in the stubbornness of their evil will, they walked in their own counsels, and looked backward rather than forward. From the day that your ancestors came out of the land of Egypt until this day, I have persistently sent all my servants the prophets to them, day after day; yet they did not listen to me, or pay attention, but they stiffened their necks. They did worse than their ancestors did.*
>
> *So you shall speak all these words to them, but they will not listen to you. You shall call to them, but they will not answer you. You shall say to them: This is the nation that did not obey the voice of the LORD their God, and did not accept discipline; truth has perished; it is cut off from their lips. (Jeremiah 7:23-28)*

This passage from the prophet Jeremiah doesn't sound like a voice of encouragement. God keeps sending prophets, and we keep refusing to listen to them. We're confronted with our own struggle and failures, our own tendencies to fall away from truth. That could easily discourage us if we didn't see that this is all part of a process of discernment that the Lord is leading us through.

I heard the story of someone who was being given a tour of an Eastern Orthodox monastery. He naively asked his guide, "So, what do you monks *do* in the monastery?" The monk answered, "We fall down, and we get up. And we fall down, and we get up. And we fall down, and we get up."

How easily to be discouraged if we did not know the encouragement, the joy, the hope that is also part of that process of learning and discerning the right path. We advance in the Spirit, we grow as human beings, by learning how to fall and rise with the Lord, united to the Lord, turning our face toward him again and again.

There is a devotional prayer service that some churches hold during Lent, usually on the Fridays of this season. It's called the "Stations of the Cross." It is a walking prayer—a brief pilgrimage, if you will—where participants stop at different "stations" or scenes along the path of Jesus' last steps. It imagines three times when Jesus fell under the weight of the cross and got up as he continued to carry it to Calvary. It is a way of expressing how Christ embraced our finiteness and struggles on our way to God.

The Lord shares this journey of life, this journey of discernment, of falling down and getting up again, with us. He shares our humanity so that we might find our way and our healing in him. And through it all, through this daily path, the kingdom of God is coming to us.

∼

The Heart

Return, O Israel, to the LORD your God,
for you have stumbled because of your iniquity.
Take words with you
and return to the LORD;
say to him,
"Take away all guilt;
accept that which is good,
and we will offer
the fruit of our lips." (Hosea 14:1-2)

We know that the experience of love is often so consoling and delightful. It fills us with warmth and exhilaration. It gives us an experience of security, of joy, a feeling of being "home." That's an important part of love.

There's another side of love, though. It's the tough and rough side. It cares so much for the other that it will do whatever is necessary for the good of the other—not the superficial good but the deep-down, spiritual good. It commits to the hard work of fostering another's healing and growth, for the other's sake, not one's own.

It wants to see the other flourish even at risk to itself. It's the love of a parent who acts in the best interest of the child even though it will make the parent unliked. It's the love of a spouse or best friend that challenges the beloved to grow, even when the beloved doesn't want to be challenged. This love is resilient and clear-sighted.

The prophets of Israel understood these different aspects of love. They glory in the comfort and abundance of God's blessings. And they confront the realities of sin and falsehood that others do not want to see or address.

The prophet Hosea is famous for his marriage problems. He married Gomer, a woman who turned away from him and his love, becoming a harlot. His faithfulness and sensitivity allowed him to see in his own personal tragedy an image of God's relationship to his people. Through their wickedness, their idolatry, their brutal oppression of the poor, the people had turned away from God. They will undergo the consequences of straying from the truth of their calling and of spurning God's appeals for restoration and renewal. Throughout most of his book, Hosea speaks out of his frustration and pain, trying to get his people to face their predicament, their rebellion in the face of God's loving intent for them.

> *When Israel was a child, I loved him,*
> *and out of Egypt I called my son.*

The more I called them,
        the more they went from me;
they kept sacrificing to the Baals,
        and offering incense to idols.
Yet it was I who taught Ephraim to walk,
        I took them up in my arms;
        but they did not know that I healed them.
I led them with cords of human kindness,
        with bands of love.
I was to them like those
        who lift infants to their cheeks.
        I bent down to them and fed them.
They shall return to the land of Egypt,
        and Assyria shall be their king,
        because they have refused to return to me.
The sword rages in their cities,
        it consumes their oracle-priests,
        and devours because of their schemes.
My people are bent on turning away from me.
        To the Most High they call,
        but he does not raise them up at all.
How can I give you up, Ephraim?
        How can I hand you over, O Israel?
How can I make you like Admah?
        How can I treat you like Zeboiim?
My heart recoils within me;
        my compassion grows warm and tender.
I will not execute my fierce anger;
        I will not again destroy Ephraim;

> *for I am God and no mortal,*
> *the Holy One in your midst,*
> *and I will not come in wrath. (Hosea 11:1-9)*

Some of the most tender verses in the Old Testament are here. Israel is a wayward child who does not know how loved he or she is. God doesn't treat his people like work animals, forcing them to obey, but leads them *"with cords of kindness, with bands of love."* God draws them with affection. *"My heart recoils within me."* God's heart is overwhelmed with compassion and warmth for his children. The way out of the sin and pain that frustrates us will be through the heart.

> *One of the scribes came near and heard them disputing with one another, and seeing that he answered them well, he asked him, "Which commandment is the first of all?" Jesus answered, "The first is, 'Hear, O Israel: the Lord our God, the Lord is one; you shall love the Lord your God with all your heart, and with all your soul, and with all your mind, and with all your strength.' The second is this, 'You shall love your neighbor as yourself.' There is no other commandment greater than these." Then the scribe said to him, "You are right, Teacher; you have truly said that 'he is one, and besides him there is no other'; and 'to love him with all the heart, and with all the understanding, and with all the strength,' and 'to love one's neighbor as oneself,' —this is much more important than all whole burnt offerings and sacrifices." When Jesus saw that he*

> *answered wisely, he said to him, "You are not far from*
> *the kingdom of God." After that no one dared to ask him*
> *any question. (Mark 12:28-34)*

Jesus also speaks of the heart. Today, we often see the heart as a symbol for the emotional side of one's life. We think of our feelings. In the Bible, the heart is more than that. It symbolizes the center of one's being. It signifies emotions, intelligence, decision-making, and the will. That's what we need to bring to the Lord: our center, our whole selves.

I heard a story once: An old pilgrim was making his way to a shrine high in the Himalayas. It was winter, and a storm was coming. He stopped in a village along the way, and the villagers tried to dissuade him from going further. The wind picked up, and more snows were coming. They asked, "What makes you think you'll even get there?" But the old man answered, "My heart is already there. It's easy for the rest of me to follow."

Are there obstacles in our lives? Are there problems we need to deal with? Are worries or fears or bad habits holding us back? Are we confused about what we should do in a particular situation? Are we struggling with what it means to love?

The question to ask is: Where is our heart? Have we placed our heart with the Lord? Do we recognize the love of God at the center of our lives? Are we seeking to respond to that love with love?

We must go to our center and let ourselves be loved there. That's how we learn to love others. The first commandment will teach us the second commandment. Loving God with our heart, soul, mind, and strength will teach us to love our neighbor. In any given situation, that may be easy, or it may be tough. It may be delightful or sacrificial. In each case, though, it will be our hearts responding to love with love.

FOUR

The Spring

He did not say: you will not be troubled, you will not be belabored, you will not be disquieted; but he said: You will not be overcome.

—Julian of Norwich, *Showings*

Light

The LORD said to Samuel, "How long will you grieve over Saul? I have rejected him from being king over Israel. Fill your horn with oil and set out; I will send you to Jesse the Bethlehemite, for I have provided for myself a king among his sons." . . . Samuel did what the LORD commanded, and came to Bethlehem. The elders of the city came to meet him trembling, and said, "Do you come peaceably?" He said, "Peaceably; I have come to sacrifice to the LORD; sanctify yourselves and come with me to the sacrifice." And he sanctified Jesse and his sons and invited them to the sacrifice.

When they came, he looked on Eliab and thought, "Surely the LORD's anointed is now before the LORD." But the LORD said to Samuel, "Do not look on his appearance or on the height of his stature, because I have rejected him; for the LORD does not see as mortals see; they look on the outward appearance, but the LORD looks on the heart." Then Jesse called Abinadab, and made him pass before Samuel. He said, "Neither has the LORD chosen this one." Then Jesse made Shammah pass by. And he said, "Neither has the LORD chosen this one." Jesse made seven of his sons pass before Samuel, and Samuel said to Jesse, "The LORD has not chosen any of these." Samuel said to Jesse, "Are all your sons here?" And he said, "There remains yet the youngest, but he is keeping the sheep." And Samuel said to Jesse, "Send and bring him; for we will not sit down until he comes here." He sent and brought him in. Now he was ruddy, and had beautiful

eyes, and was handsome. The LORD said, "Rise and
anoint him; for this is the one." Then Samuel took the
horn of oil, and anointed him in the presence of his
brothers; and the spirit of the LORD came mightily upon
David from that day forward. (1 Samuel 16:1, 4-13)

We spoke earlier of the Desert Fathers and Desert Mothers, those early Christian figures who left the cities and went out to the desert to do battle with evil. Their stories were meant to teach some wisdom about discipleship. A story is told of Abba Elias, who one night was battling a particularly obstinate demon. After several prayers of exorcism, the demon was still tormenting him and started dragging him across the ground. Finally, Elias prayed "Jesus, save me!" and the demon fled. Elias, though, returned home angry. The Lord spoke to him and asked, "What's wrong now?" Elias replied, "You did not answer my first prayers, but allowed the demon to drag me on the ground." The Lord answered, "Why were you worried? As soon as you looked, you saw I was by your side."

"As soon as you looked." There is looking, and then there is looking. There is seeing, and then there is really seeing. If you want to be a disciple, you will have to really see. That is what will get you through the hard times, the times when it seems that evil is flourishing while the good are dragged across the ground. That is what will show you that you're not alone, that the Lord is always by your side.

God sent Samuel to the house of Jesse to anoint a king. Some may have looked at David, the youngest son of Jesse, and seen nothing special, someone who could easily be passed over. Samuel looked and saw God's chosen. When we begin to see with God's eyes, we see more than the outward appearance of people and events. We see the heart of things. We can change the direction of our lives. The spirit begins to flow mightily. A new journey begins.

A young man, a college football player, came to see me once to talk about something that was happening in his life. In the course of two months, he lost his two best friends. One was killed in a car accident. The other died swimming in the ocean, not far from shore. This young man thought that he could handle this loss well on his own. He wanted to be strong for his friends' families. Everyone was telling him that he needed to continue to live and study and compete for his friends, in their memory. His outward appearance remained sturdy.

Then things started to fall apart. He had no more interest in doing well in his classes. He stopped going to practice. He started to withdraw from people. He told me how he would drive alone sometimes, and then stop in the middle of nowhere and start to sob uncontrollably. Why were his best friends taken and he left behind? Why did their families have to suffer, but not his? He felt lost and didn't know how long he could go on trying to be strong for others.

At one point I asked him if he was familiar with the classic "stages of grief" first explored by Elisabeth

Kübler-Ross, a nurse and hospice worker.[5] He remembered them from a class he once took: denial, bargaining, anger, depression, and then acceptance. We talked about these in his own experience. They were no longer concepts in a textbook for him. They were ways of coming to grips with his loss and trying to understand the mystery of his life's path. He was willing to travel that path out his current darkness. He was willing to grasp God's purpose, God's need, for him. He was willing to see.

> *For once you were darkness, but now in the Lord you are light. Live as children of light— for the fruit of the light is found in all that is good and right and true. Try to find out what is pleasing to the Lord. Take no part in the unfruitful works of darkness, but instead expose them. For it is shameful even to mention what such people do secretly; but everything exposed by the light becomes visible, for everything that becomes visible is light. Therefore it says,*
>
> > *"Sleeper, awake!*
> > *Rise from the dead,*
> > *and Christ will shine on you." (Ephesians 5:8-14)*

Light makes sight possible. Light guides our path out of darkness. It allows us to look, to see, to really understand. There is something within us that is ready to receive that light. We can't produce it on our own, but we can place ourselves in its beam. We can pray for it to shine on us and to flood our path with light.

We can welcome the Lord's work in us. No matter what darkness we may face, the light is with us. We simply have to look and see that the Lord is always by our side. There is nothing to fear. His light embraces us, heals us, and makes us children of the light.

~

Sight

As he walked along, he saw a man blind from birth. His disciples asked him, "Rabbi, who sinned, this man or his parents, that he was born blind?" Jesus answered, "Neither this man nor his parents sinned; he was born blind so that God's works might be revealed in him. We must work the works of him who sent me while it is day; night is coming when no one can work. As long as I am in the world, I am the light of the world." When he had said this, he spat on the ground and made mud with the saliva and spread the mud on the man's eyes, saying to him, "Go, wash in the pool of Siloam" (which means Sent). Then he went and washed and came back able to see. (John 9:1-7)

There are videos on YouTube that show the moment when people who have been blind or visually impaired for most of their lives, or even from birth, first receive the gift of sight. They've had operations to correct their vision and are suddenly able to see. We witness the bandages coming off their eyes and the reactions from them and the people around them. These are truly astonishing and heartwarming moments.

You may know the book *Pilgrim at Tinker Creek* by Annie Dillard.[6] As one of her first books, it established her as an author who could look at the smallest, commonest things in nature and see metaphors for the largest questions of life. In one of the chapters she relates stories from surgeons who had discovered how to perform safe operations on people who had been blinded by cataracts from birth. These were adults and children from around the world. It's a fascinating history.

Imagine never having experienced the sense of sight and suddenly having it thrust upon you. Imagine having to deal with all this new information about the world. Things that people with sight rarely think about had to be learned step-by-step. What most children learn as they crawl around the living room, or when someone plays "peek a boo" with them, had to be reasoned through with great effort.

One girl loved the sensation of color but didn't understand the dark spots amid the flat patches of color she saw. She had to learn the meaning of shadows and how they disclose depth and form. A boy kept bumping into the color patches until he learned that they had substance and that he needed to put his sense of touch and sight together. A man, after weeks, was still struggling with how to estimate distances and how to maneuver through space and color. A woman was frightened by a staircase, not able to decipher its visual cues. For the newly sighted, their previously manageable and touchable worlds became tremendously large and complex. They would retreat at times by closing their eyes.

Yet, Dillard writes, they delighted in the smallest things this visual world opened up to them. One man, when the bandages first came off, was astonished by his own hands and fingers. He was amazed at how different human faces were. A young woman gazed at everything around her and just kept repeating: "O God, how beautiful." In one of those YouTube videos, a young man, seeing color for the first time, sits on the grass and just looks down at it, astonished, saying: "It's so beautiful."

> *They brought to the Pharisees the man who had formerly been blind. Now it was a sabbath day when Jesus made the mud and opened his eyes. Then the Pharisees also began to ask him how he had received his sight. He said to them, "He put mud on my eyes. Then I washed, and now I see." Some of the Pharisees said, "This man is not from God, for he does not observe the sabbath." But others said, "How can a man who is a sinner perform such signs?" And they were divided. So they said again to the blind man, "What do you say about him? It was your eyes he opened." He said, "He is a prophet." (John 9:13-17)*

Christian tradition, from the Scriptures onward, has groped for images and words to describe the experience of divine life among us, the experience of Christ. We search for a way to speak about what life in Christ means. But it goes beyond words, so we turn to metaphors and stories.

That is why the gospel of John spends so much time with the story of the man born blind. It is, as John often calls Jesus' miracles, a "sign." It is a sign of what Christ brings to the world. Jesus opens us up to life in a new way. He brings a new dimension, a new depth. It is as radical a change as what this man experiences, seeing the world for the first time. Now we can see, not just as humans see, but as God sees. We see what is most real. We see beyond appearances. We see with the heart.

The light for this kind of seeing is all around us. And it changes the way we see. We see others differently. We stop judging people by the way they look, or what they have. We begin to see others as they are, in their uniqueness. We begin to respect others and learn from them in new ways, appreciating the mystery they carry within.

We see ourselves differently, too. We stop judging ourselves according to what others think of us. We begin to see ourselves as God sees us, as we are, as we are loved. And so we become more loving toward ourselves and more free to change.

We see life differently. It's no longer about choosing sides, or using others, or hoarding things. It's not something we have to fight, or something we must endure. We see life as a gift. We savor it. We begin to use it differently. Life becomes an adventure. It offers one opportunity after another.

This way of seeing changes everything. It doesn't mean that life becomes easy. There may still be hardship, pain, and suffering; but because we are different, they will not defeat us. Even there we'll see the seeds of growth. And we'll know that we're not alone.

Helen Keller, unable to see or hear from childhood, once said, "I have been given so much. I have no time to consider what has been withheld." She saw. She had sight.

> *So for the second time they called the man who had been blind, and they said to him, "Give glory to God! We know that this man is a sinner." He answered, "I do not know whether he is a sinner. One thing I do know, that though I was blind, now I see." They said to him, "What did he do to you? How did he open your eyes?" He answered them, "I have told you already, and you would not listen. Why do you want to hear it again? Do you also want to become his disciples?" Then they reviled him, saying, "You are his disciple, but we are disciples of Moses. We know that God has spoken to Moses, but as for this man, we do not know where he comes from." The man answered, "Here is an astonishing thing! You do not know where he comes from, and yet he opened my eyes. We know that God does not listen to sinners, but he does listen to one who worships him and obeys his will. Never since the world began has it been heard that anyone opened the eyes of a person born blind. If this man were not from God, he could do nothing." They answered him, "You were born entirely in sins, and are you trying to teach us?" And they drove him out. (John 9:24-34)*

The light may be all around us, but there are times when we retreat into the darkness. How can that be? We may not want the responsibility that comes with sight, with seeing things differently. We may not want to let go of those things that give us security: the standards of the world around us, the prejudices that keep us satisfied. Even the fears can be comforting in some way. We become like those cataract patients who shut their eyes because the light is too much to handle. Pretty soon life becomes dull, colorless. We pass a tree and see only a tree. We pass a person and see only another face. But, the light to see what is real, the light that brings color, a new vision to our lives, is still there. The light of the world still beckons.

> *Jesus heard that they had driven him out, and when he found him, he said, "Do you believe in the Son of Man?" He answered, "And who is he, sir? Tell me, so that I may believe in him." Jesus said to him, "You have seen him, and the one speaking with you is he." He said, "Lord, I believe." And he worshiped him. Jesus said, "I came into this world for judgment so that those who do not see may see, and those who do see may become blind." Some of the Pharisees near him heard this and said to him, "Surely we are not blind, are we?" Jesus said to them, "If you were blind, you would not have sin. But now that you say, 'We see,' your sin remains." (John 9:35-41)*

The man in the gospel story wasn't even looking for a healing. But a light broke through. The light of the world searched him out to give the gift.

That light shines around us in simple ways. It can be seen in ordinary folks who experience a wonder about life. We see it in people who build friendships and families and futures around a vision of love, respect, and openness. We see it in those who reach out in compassion to others who are hurting, or who join together to try to heal the world. And we see it when we gather as a church to celebrate the life and light that has been poured out to us in Jesus.

~

Exile

All the leading priests and the people also were exceedingly unfaithful, following all the abominations of the nations; and they polluted the house of the LORD that he had consecrated in Jerusalem.

The LORD, the God of their ancestors, sent persistently to them by his messengers, because he had compassion on his people and on his dwelling place; but they kept mocking the messengers of God, despising his words, and scoffing at his prophets, until the wrath of the LORD against his people became so great that there was no remedy.

Therefore he brought up against them the king of the Chaldeans, who killed their youths with the sword in the house of their sanctuary, and had no compassion on young man or young woman, the aged or the feeble;

he gave them all into his hand. All the vessels of the house
of God, large and small, and the treasures of the house
of the LORD, and the treasures of the king and of his
officials, all these he brought to Babylon. They burned the
house of God, broke down the wall of Jerusalem, burned
all its palaces with fire, and destroyed all its precious
vessels. He took into exile in Babylon those who had
escaped from the sword, and they became servants to him
and to his sons until the establishment of the kingdom
of Persia, to fulfill the word of the LORD by the mouth of
Jeremiah, until the land had made up for its sabbaths.
All the days that it lay desolate it kept sabbath, to fulfill
seventy years. (2 Chronicles 36:14-21)

Exile is such an exotic word. When we hear it, we may
think of ancient history. We think of the Babylonians
burning the temple and forcing the chosen people from
their homes. Or we may think of the stories of refugees
fleeing wars in our own day. Does it seem far removed
from us? But there are many forms of exile, banishment,
separation from home.

When I taught at Yale, I discovered a small chapel in
one of the libraries known as the Nouwen Chapel. It
was named for the well-known spiritual writer Henri
Nouwen, who taught at the divinity school. I'm told he
was well liked and enjoyed his time there. But at a certain point he felt that life was getting too comfortable.
He had worked at elite universities in the developed
world, but now he felt a different call. He decided to
live in a poor village in Peru. What he heard about it

made him apprehensive. It was not a stable place, and he knew he would be encountering an unfamiliar level of poverty and disease. He wasn't sure what to expect.

In his book *¡Gracias!* about his experiences there,[7] Nouwen tells us what he found when he joined that community: laughing children, generous hospitality, trustworthy people who gathered together in families and churches, authentic people who shared so much life together. They welcomed him into their home. There was nothing to fear.

It was when he returned to his affluent, first-world friends that he noticed something different. He noticed a heaviness. Here were people who had everything—the best healthcare, education, security—yet they seemed so burdened. They were not at home in their world. They felt alienated in their communities. Their churches were divided into factions. They felt threatened at work, strained in relationships. They didn't even seem at home in their own bodies.

Perhaps the contrast seems too stark. No doubt it is colored by the intensity of Nouwen's experience. But we can still examine our own experiences of alienation. Are we at home in our world? In our community? Or, do we avoid certain people, certain neighborhoods? Do we fail to work together on common problems? In our church, are we discouraged by the discrepancies we see between our ideals and realities, or by our failure to practice the reconciliation we preach?

Are we at home with one another? Or, does fear or suspicion keep us apart? Do barriers of mistrust strain our relationships? Is our work motivated by an un-healthy kind of competition that breeds hostility? Are we at home with ourselves? Or do we spend our energy wishing we had others' qualities while discounting our own? Do we feel alienated from our bodies, anxiously refusing to allow the years to carry us along? Are we at home with God? Or do we fear that God may banish us, abandon us in our weakness, or forsake us in our deepest need?

> *In the first year of King Cyrus of Persia, in fulfillment of the word of the LORD spoken by Jeremiah, the LORD stirred up the spirit of King Cyrus of Persia so that he sent a herald throughout all his kingdom and also declared in a written edict: "Thus says King Cyrus of Persia: The LORD, the God of heaven, has given me all the kingdoms of the earth, and he has charged me to build him a house at Jerusalem, which is in Judah. Whoever is among you of all his people, may the LORD his God be with him! Let him go up." (2 Chronicles 36:22-23)*

Have you ever prayed, "God, where are you?" The cho-sen people, in their pain, their exile, may have offered that prayer. They didn't understand what was happening to them. But they never forgot their home. By looking into their history, searching through the pain, they found an answer. God had not abandoned them. God was there, in exile with them. God was there, fulfilling the words of the prophets, guiding history, preparing them for something new.

When the Persian king, Cyrus, allowed them to return to their land, their faith was shaken but still there. In fact, it was stronger as they learned new lessons and gained spiritual insights. God's presence came to them in the midst of their suffering and gave them the courage to endure. And God opened the way home.

> *But God, who is rich in mercy, out of the great love with which he loved us even when we were dead through our trespasses, made us alive together with Christ—by grace you have been saved—and raised us up with him and seated us with him in the heavenly places in Christ Jesus, so that in the ages to come he might show the immeasurable riches of his grace in kindness toward us in Christ Jesus. For by grace you have been saved through faith, and this is not your own doing; it is the gift of God—not the result of works, so that no one may boast. For we are what he has made us, created in Christ Jesus for good works, which God prepared beforehand to be our way of life. (Ephesians 2:4-10)*

As God's people we, too, search our history and find God at work. In our exiles we, too, find that God's grace has entered the darkness of alienation and sin, our human weakness and brokenness, and has brought the *"immeasurable riches of his grace"* through Christ. God entered our history in a way that can never be erased. God sent his Son so that we can believe in his love and be transformed by it. He went into exile with us, so that we can find our way home.

So in a world that stills exiles people, we will be those who welcome the exile, who bring compassion and respect to others. In communities that are divided, we will bring openness and healing. In work environments, we'll model cooperation and fairness. In our churches, we'll model the reconciliation we talk about. In all our relationships, we can allow others to feel at home. And we will be at home with ourselves, too, as we welcome God's peace within.

No matter how dark things get in life, no matter how we may feel exiled, we have nothing to fear. The God of love has made a home with us.

~

Prodigal

Then Jesus said, "There was a man who had two sons. The younger of them said to his father, 'Father, give me the share of the property that will belong to me.' So he divided his property between them. A few days later the younger son gathered all he had and traveled to a distant country, and there he squandered his property in dissolute living. When he had spent everything, a severe famine took place throughout that country, and he began to be in need. So he went and hired himself out to one of the citizens of that country, who sent him to his fields to feed the pigs. He would gladly have filled himself with the pods that the pigs were eating; and no one gave him

*anything. But when he came to himself he said, 'How
many of my father's hired hands have bread enough and
to spare, but here I am dying of hunger! I will get up and
go to my father, and I will say to him, "Father, I have
sinned against heaven and before you; I am no longer
worthy to be called your son; treat me like one of your
hired hands."' So he set off and went to his father. But
while he was still far off, his father saw him and was filled
with compassion; he ran and put his arms around him
and kissed him. Then the son said to him, 'Father, I have
sinned against heaven and before you; I am no longer
worthy to be called your son.' But the father said to his
slaves, 'Quickly, bring out a robe—the best one—and put
it on him; put a ring on his finger and sandals on his feet.
And get the fatted calf and kill it, and let us eat and
celebrate; for this son of mine was dead and is alive again;
he was lost and is found!' And they began to celebrate.*

*"Now his elder son was in the field; and when he
came and approached the house, he heard music and
dancing. He called one of the slaves and asked what was
going on. He replied, 'Your brother has come, and your
father has killed the fatted calf, because he has got him
back safe and sound.' Then he became angry and refused
to go in. His father came out and began to plead with
him. But he answered his father, 'Listen! For all these
years I have been working like a slave for you, and I have
never disobeyed your command; yet you have never given
me even a young goat so that I might celebrate with my
friends. But when this son of yours came back, who has
devoured your property with prostitutes, you killed the*

fatted calf for him!' Then the father said to him, 'Son,
you are always with me, and all that is mine is yours.
But we had to celebrate and rejoice, because this brother
of yours was dead and has come to life; he was lost and
has been found.'" (Luke 15:11-32)

When I ask my students to define the word "prodigal," I usually get some good guesses. But they tend to be wrong. Your thesaurus will provide you with the usual synonyms: "reckless," "extravagant," "wasteful," "lavish," "luxuriant," "profuse." It's enough to make you want to go out and be prodigal!

And that wouldn't be a bad thing. We're used to calling this passage the parable of the Prodigal Son. But some prefer to call it the parable of the Prodigal Father.[8] He's the extravagant one. He recklessly wastes his love and mercy, lavishing it on his children.

The two brothers we meet may be different, but they also have a lot in common. Both of them fail to recognize how much they are loved. They don't realize how profuse their father's love for them is, how precious they are in his sight. Neither sees the way the father sees, and that's the source of their problems.

The first son, the younger one, thinks that if he returns to his father's house, he'll have to grovel and become one of the hired hands. He doesn't grasp that his father would be waiting, hoping for his return. He can't imagine that his father would be going out each day and looking for him, ready to welcome him back to life.

This son has been prodigal, because he's wasted himself—his time, talent, life, potential—on what was not worthy of him. He only hurt himself by throwing away the gifts he'd been given. But it would be better to be like this son, since, as we are told, he "*came to himself.*" He came to his senses. Through pain, he learned from his mistakes. He wanted a way out.

The way out for him will be the way out for us—seeing ourselves as the Lord sees us. Seeing our gifts. Coming to know how precious we are in God's sight.

The second son, the older one, is prodigal in a different way. But we don't know if he comes to his senses or not, since the story ends. Our first thought might be to sympathize with this son who feels unappreciated. But that's not his problem; he has a tougher issue to deal with. He doesn't realize how loved he is, either. His father tells him, "*You are always with me, and all that is mine is yours.*" It's all yours, he's told.

This kid could've asked for a party anytime! But, more than that, he had his father's presence. He was surrounded by his father's love and devotion, but he didn't see it, either. If he did, he probably would've been out there on the road with his dad, waiting and hoping for his brother's return. He's wasting his life, too, but in a different way. He's wasting it in his stinginess, envy, self-righteousness, and resentment. He might as well have been out feeding the pigs, too, for all the good it did him to be home.

Can we relate to this brother, too? There's a banquet going on, and he's refusing to go in. Here we are, surrounded by signs that tells us of our Father's love. Has it changed us? Freed us?

There are ways we can be like the older brother. We can talk about a religion of love, and then go around hating ourselves. We can create a religion of dos and don'ts, but not be free enough to go beyond the rules to do good. We can be consumed by envy of what others have and spend our time hoarding things that have little real value. We can stay at home, safe and hidden, and never go out and meet new challenges of growth.

It's only by being prodigal that we will discover how rich we are, how loved we are, how precious life is. That's what frees us to see our own worth, to be generous, to go out on the road and welcome others home.

So what kind of prodigal will we be? We can't become like the prodigal father on our own. We can't make it happen on our own steam. We can just do what the prodigal son did: We can welcome it. We can allow the Lord to lavish us with his love. Then our eyes can be opened. We can come to our senses and realize how precious this gift is. And we will be freed to love others into that kingdom that Jesus told such beautiful stories about.

The Font

When I lived in Texas, a favorite pastime in the hot weather was to go "tubing." The way people described it to me, however, made the activity sound a little ambiguous. People would float in large rubber tubes down tranquil streams, enjoying the comfort of a lazy afternoon. Floating nearby would be another tube that held cold (usually fermented) refreshments. As one sailed along, however, there was the chance of intermittent harrowing experiences. The water could suddenly become agitated while the tube got tossed around. You could suddenly feel like you're riding the rapids, not sure if you'd be thrown into the water. It's those exciting moments, though, that the "tubers" looked forward to. They found the contrasting moods and risky uncertainty fun and exhilarating.

Might this offer another image of the spiritual life? Sometimes we need the experience of floating peacefully down the tranquil waters of life. We're aware that the Lord is holding us in the palm of his hand, offering us a peaceful balm. At other times, the Lord is splashing us with his grace, challenging us with powerful currents and uncertain outcomes. We must wake up and hold on.

> *After this there was a festival of the Jews, and Jesus went up to Jerusalem.*
>
> *Now in Jerusalem by the Sheep Gate there is a pool, called in Hebrew Beth-zatha, which has five porticoes.*

*In these lay many invalids—blind, lame, and paralyzed.
One man was there who had been ill for thirty-eight years.
When Jesus saw him lying there and knew that he had
been there a long time, he said to him, "Do you want to
be made well?" The sick man answered him, "Sir, I have
no one to put me into the pool when the water is stirred
up; and while I am making my way, someone else steps
down ahead of me." Jesus said to him, "Stand up, take
your mat and walk." At once the man was made well,
and he took up his mat and began to walk.*
 Now that day was a sabbath. (John 5:1-9)

There is a man sitting by a pool in Jerusalem, a pool that
is purported to have healing properties (this is a holy
city, after all). Apparently, a hidden spring intermittently
bubbles up and disturbs the water, and people want to
enter the pool at that time. But this man can never get
there, because no one will help him. So he just keeps
waiting. Maybe he's become comfortable on the sidelines. Maybe he's making a living just complaining about
how unfortunate he is, begging for scraps. But Jesus will
have none of that. *"Stand up, take your mat and walk."*

 Jesus is the font. He is the spring of water who brings
healing grace. And he will have none of our feelings of
dependency, despondency, or victimhood. He comes to
us and says: "Get up!" We may not always want to hear
that. We'd rather keep floating by undisturbed. We'd
rather complain. Are we afraid of getting splashed? Are
we uncertain that we have what it takes to follow his

lead? He comes and says: "Get up! Claim your power. I'm the one who gives it to you. Now act on it."

To hear that word is exhilarating. It means getting splashed and waking up. But it is also risky. We must act on it—and keep acting on it.

We're told that Jesus encounters the man from the pool again:

> *Later Jesus found him in the temple and said to him,*
> *"See, you have been made well! Do not sin any more,*
> *so that nothing worse happens to you." (John 5:14)*

How easy it is for us to fall back into our unhealthy habits, to return to our dependencies and victimhood. Don't go back, Jesus tells us. We must keep walking in the faith and power that he gives. The water we receive from him, the healing of our self-understanding, will renew us. It will give us vitality and affect the way we relate to others. But we must stay awake. We need to keep walking in faith.

> *Then he brought me back to the entrance of the temple;*
> *there, water was flowing from below the threshold of the*
> *temple toward the east (for the temple faced east); and*
> *the water was flowing down from below the south end of*
> *the threshold of the temple, south of the altar. Then he*
> *brought me out by way of the north gate, and led me*
> *around on the outside to the outer gate that faces toward*
> *the east; and the water was coming out on the south side.*

Going on eastward with a cord in his hand, the man measured one thousand cubits, and then led me through the water; and it was ankle-deep. Again he measured one thousand, and led me through the water; and it was knee-deep. Again he measured one thousand, and led me through the water; and it was up to the waist. Again he measured one thousand, and it was a river that I could not cross, for the water had risen; it was deep enough to swim in, a river that could not be crossed. He said to me, "Mortal, have you seen this?"

Then he led me back along the bank of the river. As I came back, I saw on the bank of the river a great many trees on the one side and on the other. He said to me, "This water flows toward the eastern region and goes down into the Arabah; and when it enters the sea, the sea of stagnant waters, the water will become fresh. Wherever the river goes, every living creature that swarms will live, and there will be very many fish, once these waters reach there. It will become fresh; and everything will live where the river goes. People will stand fishing beside the sea from En-gedi to En-eglaim; it will be a place for the spreading of nets; its fish will be of a great many kinds, like the fish of the Great Sea. But its swamps and marshes will not become fresh; they are to be left for salt. On the banks, on both sides of the river, there will grow all kinds of trees for food. Their leaves will not wither nor their fruit fail, but they will bear fresh fruit every month, because the water for them flows from the sanctuary. Their fruit will be for food, and their leaves for healing." (Ezekiel 47:1-12)

Water flows throughout the Bible. It courses from the primordial waters of chaos in Genesis, to the life-giving waters streaming through the new Jerusalem as depicted in the book of Revelation. The symbolic power of water is heightened for a desert people.

In the passage above, the prophet Ezekiel is given a vision of a restored temple. From every side of the temple, living water springs. It becomes a mighty river, irrigating the land, making it verdant and fruitful. Spiritual directors and pastors often refer to this passage as it can relate to prayer. I was on a retreat once where the director stated simply: "The temple is the soul."

How is your prayer life going? Are you in an oasis or a desert? In either case, you can remember the temple that is your soul. The font is within. Even in the dryness, in the lack of feeling or consolation, the stress of work and rocky relationships, it is an unfailing font, a font of living water. It will flow from your center to the dry land. You will find food and salt, nourishment and medicine.

Very often people tell me that they aren't finding enough time for prayer. They know it's important, and they want to carve out more time in their day for prayer, but it doesn't happen. Sometimes, I try to reframe their understanding of the time they seek, the quality of that time. I say: Don't put prayer on your "to do" list. Often in the midst of our stress and work, if prayer is just another thing we "have' to do, it quickly falls to the bottom of the list. The end of the day comes, we're too tired, and now we feel guilty about it, too. Prayer has become "work." The discipline of prayer has become the discipline of work.

Try this: Instead of making prayer another item on the "to do" list, see prayer as the time in your day when you get to let go of that list. It's the time when you get to let go of work and take time for yourself and God. What do you enjoy? Take time for that as a way to refresh yourself during the day—and do that with the Lord. Any activity can become prayer. Art, music, walking in nature. Take that walk with the Lord. Instead of rushing from one appointment to another, walk calmly and be aware of all that is around you. It will speak to your spirit. Something tells me that if we see these times in our day as prayer, we will find more and more time for prayer. We will look forward to prayer as the time when we can let go and enjoy God's presence with us.

Wherever we are, the font is there. Are we on the sidelines, feeling powerless? We can count on it to splash us in the face and wake us up. Are we stressed? It will bring refreshment and healing. Are we at the oasis? We can let ourselves float on that peaceful current. The font is there. The Lord is there.

Adversaries

Jesus said to them, "Very truly, I tell you, the Son can do nothing on his own, but only what he sees the Father

> *doing; for whatever the Father does, the Son does likewise. The Father loves the Son and shows him all that he himself is doing; and he will show him greater works than these, so that you will be astonished. Indeed, just as the Father raises the dead and gives them life, so also the Son gives life to whomever he wishes." (John 5:19-21)*

This passage comes right after the healing we read about above. Jesus told the man by the pool in Jerusalem: *"Stand up, take your mat and walk."* After years of dejection and gloom, he is now a walking sign of God's healing, God's power over passivity and loss. Now he is in charge of his mat. He's in charge of where he goes.

Yet St. John tells us this happened on a Sabbath. The legal authorities see the man carrying his mat, a type of work that is not approved for the Sabbath, and so, we are told, they begin to persecute Jesus. They become his adversaries, plotting against him. Jesus is not unique in this regard. All the prophets of Israel had their detractors. Human beings don't want what is familiar to them to be challenged. They don't want their ideologies questioned. A man had just been healed; he was a walking prayer of praise. But to these adversaries, religious ideas were more important. Even a divine act cannot move them.

The passage above shows how Jesus responds to those who oppose his work. First, he stands within his own relationship to God, his own identity. He knows that he is the Son of the Father in a unique sense. He stands in that intimacy with God and in his call to do the Father's will. Just as God acts on the Sabbath, sustaining life and giving life, so Jesus will heal and give life on the Sabbath. Jesus knows who he is and what he is here to do.

He continues to respond:

> *"You search the scriptures because you think that in them you have eternal life; and it is they that testify on my behalf. Yet you refuse to come to me to have life. I do not accept glory from human beings. But I know that you do not have the love of God in you. I have come in my Father's name, and you do not accept me; if another comes in his own name, you will accept him. How can you believe when you accept glory from one another and do not seek the glory that comes from the one who alone is God? Do not think that I will accuse you before the Father; your accuser is Moses, on whom you have set your hope. If you believed Moses, you would believe me, for he wrote about me. But if you do not believe what he wrote, how will you believe what I say?" (John 5:39-47)*

Jesus makes the distinction between seeking human regard, human "glory," and seeking the glory that comes from God. He points his detractors to the Scriptures. They think they know God's law, but their knowledge is superficial. They must go deeper. They must understand the law on another level. They must go beyond the letter of the law to the heart of the law. When they do, they will see that Jesus is doing what Moses did, that he is fulfilling what Moses taught.

We may not have to deal with the same kind of opposition that the prophets endured, but we will certainly know what it is like to deal with difficult people, or even adversaries. There are those who will refuse to listen to what we say. They may not even try to understand where we are coming from. There are those who will attempt to undermine our efforts or badmouth us at work. How might we respond? First, we will have to be humble. We aren't necessarily a prophet in every instance. We might have to listen to others, and reexamine our positions, plans, or methods. How are we contributing to misunderstanding, or failing to communicate honestly? We may need to purify our own motives.

Yet, when we sincerely follow our path of discipleship and are confident in our motives, we take the lead from Jesus. We must stand in our relationship to the Lord and all he has shown us. We don't back down from our call to heal and give life to those we lead or those we serve. We are also free to challenge others to go deeper in their understanding of the spiritual truths that inspire us to act. We stay true to ourselves and let the cards fall where they will.

> *The LORD said to Moses, "Go down at once! Your people, whom you brought up out of the land of Egypt, have acted perversely; they have been quick to turn aside from the way that I commanded them; they have cast for themselves an image of a calf, and have worshiped it and sacrificed to it, and said, 'These are your gods, O Israel,*

*who brought you up out of the land of Egypt!'" The L*ORD
said to Moses, "I have seen this people, how stiff-necked
they are. Now let me alone, so that my wrath may burn
hot against them and I may consume them; and of you
I will make a great nation."

*But Moses implored the L*ORD *his God, and said,*
*"O L*ORD*, why does your wrath burn hot against your*
people, whom you brought out of the land of Egypt with
great power and with a mighty hand? Why should the
Egyptians say, 'It was with evil intent that he brought
them out to kill them in the mountains, and to consume
them from the face of the earth'? Turn from your fierce
wrath; change your mind and do not bring disaster on
your people. Remember Abraham, Isaac, and Israel, your
servants, how you swore to them by your own self, saying
to them, 'I will multiply your descendants like the stars of
heaven, and all this land that I have promised I will give
to your descendants, and they shall inherit it forever.'"
*And the L*ORD *changed his mind about the disaster that*
he planned to bring on his people. (Exodus 32:7-14)

In this passage, Moses is on Mt. Sinai, ready to bring the
law to his people, but they have already turned away
from God. God is ready to wipe them out right there in
the desert. But then we have the famous prayer of
Moses, asking God to relent in punishing the people for
their sins.

Did God need to be reminded by Moses of his promises to Abraham, Isaac, and Jacob? Did God need to be

reminded that he is compassionate? Or was this God's way of reminding Moses? Was this God's way of coaxing out of Moses the realization that these people, even with all their weaknesses and faults, were still the Lord's chosen, still part of God's plan? Was it Moses, in his own weakness and readiness to give up on these people, who needed to be reminded that God was not giving up on them?

There may be adversaries to deal with in life. We must be clear about the truth as we see it and seek it. We must also be humble and open-minded with others. We choose not to respond to bad behavior in kind, but in charity, knowing that we all have our strengths and weaknesses and that we're all in this together.

We are part of God's plan, and God is strong enough to bring his plan to fruition as we seek his way in our lives. God will not give up on us, so why should we?

$\sim$

Lifted Up

From Mount Hor they set out by the way to the Red Sea, to go around the land of Edom; but the people became impatient on the way. The people spoke against God and against Moses, "Why have you brought us up out of Egypt to die in the wilderness? For there is no food and no water, and we detest this miserable food." Then the LORD sent poisonous serpents among the people, and they bit the people, so that many Israelites died. The people came to Moses and said, "We have sinned by speaking against the LORD and against you; pray to the LORD to take away the serpents from us." So Moses prayed for the people. And the LORD said to Moses, "Make a poisonous serpent, and set it on a pole; and everyone who is bitten shall look at it and live." So Moses made a serpent of bronze, and put it upon a pole; and whenever a serpent bit someone, that person would look at the serpent of bronze and live. (Numbers 21:4-9)

Again, Moses is in the role of having to pray to God for these wayward people. They have sinned and are now experiencing the consequences of sin. Distrust and rebellion result in pain and suffering. Curiously, Moses is instructed to make an image that represents the causes of this pain and lift it up for all to see. When viewed by the people, this becomes a path of healing.

What is going on in this story? The Scriptures stand firmly against the use of magic in cultic practices, so that has no place in understanding this event. It is clear that God is the agent of healing here, not a primitive totem. When the people are told to look at the bronze serpent, what are they being called to witness? What are they being invited to see?

How often do we fail to make the connections between our sin and our suffering? The world around us tells us to look out only for ourselves. It teaches us to lash out and attack. Our failure to listen, our need to dominate, our desire for revenge—there are so many ways we can harm others and break down community. Are we aware of how our selfishness, fear, and lack of forgiveness defeats our own desires? How our sin hurts ourselves?

Moses raises up the serpent. Is he giving his people a chance to make the connection between their disordered lives and their pain? Are they being invited to come to a deeper awareness of how God's law, God's way, will bring them healing and a new life? Look at the consequences of how you are thinking and what you are doing. Make the connections. Be open to a new awareness. You are opening the door for God's healing.

> *And just as Moses lifted up the serpent in the wilderness, so must the Son of Man be lifted up, that whoever believes in him may have eternal life.*
>
> *"For God so loved the world that he gave his only Son, so that everyone who believes in him may not perish but may have eternal life.*
>
> *"Indeed, God did not send the Son into the world to condemn the world, but in order that the world might be saved through him. Those who believe in him are not condemned; but those who do not believe are condemned already, because they have not believed in the name of the only Son of God. And this is the judgment, that the light has come into the world, and people loved darkness rather than light because their deeds were evil. For all who do*

> *evil hate the light and do not come to the light, so that*
> *their deeds may not be exposed. But those who do what is*
> *true come to the light, so that it may be clearly seen that*
> *their deeds have been done in God." (John 3:14-21)*

When Jesus speaks of being "lifted up" in John's gospel, it refers to his crucifixion. Many, when they look at the image of the cross, see only wood. We see a sign of hope, healing, and promise. Some look and see an instrument of pain, torture, and death. We see God's light overcoming darkness and anything that seeks our destruction. We see the triumph of God's love over the consequences of sin. When we believe in this love, the door to a new, redeemed life opens for us.

> *So Jesus said, "When you have lifted up the Son of Man,*
> *then you will realize that I am he, and that I do nothing*
> *on my own, but I speak these things as the Father*
> *instructed me. And the one who sent me is with me;*
> *he has not left me alone, for I always do what is pleasing*
> *to him." As he was saying these things, many believed in*
> *him. (John 8:28-30)*

Here in the eighth chapter of John's gospel, Jesus is speaking to his opponents, but then things change with the last verse of the passage. As Jesus speaks, many believe. People are offered the gift of faith, so that they can look upon the one who has been lifted up and find healing.

On this road to Jerusalem, we are asked again and again to see beyond appearances, to look beyond the superficial. God is lurking everywhere when we have the eyes to see. As our path in life intersects Jesus' path, we prepare to see God's purpose for us in a new way.

FIVE

The Stone

I must keep alive in myself the desire for my true country, which I shall not find till after death; I must never let it get snowed under or turned aside; I must make it the main object of life to press on to that other country and to help others to do the same.

—C. S. Lewis, *Mere Christianity*

The Code

One way that scholars have found evidence for how Christianity spread in the ancient world is through inscriptions left on public monuments, such as graves. Marble slabs in cemeteries would carry symbols and epitaphs that at times indicated religious identity. For example, the earliest Christian graves might have small symbols like a fish (for Christ), an anchor (hope), or a palm (victory).

Before the fourth century, because of persecutions, Christian epitaphs could not be as open or candid in the use of language. A kind of code may have been used to signal Christian meaning. For example, the inscription for a second-century bishop in Asia Minor named Abercius speaks of him as "a disciple of a holy shepherd." It speaks of a great fish caught by a "holy virgin" that gives food under the forms of bread and wine. It asks those who can "discern these things" to pray for him.

I've been told of another fragment of an ancient epitaph that reads: "he was forty-seven years old, but he really lived seven years." This, it is thought, signified that the man was baptized seven years before his death. Christians passing by who knew the code would stop and offer a prayer.

Would we understand the meaning of that code? Someone is saying that he met Christ, he was baptized, and his life was changed. He really started living. He came alive in a new way. What could this mean? Life somehow meant more to him now. There was new joy, new peace in life. He had a sense of direction or purpose. Or he was able to forgive himself. Or he learned how to open himself to love others. Or whatever it was—Christ brought him to life. He began to see life in a new way.

Could we walk by that grave and say, "Oh, yeah, we get it. We know what the Lord can do in someone's life." There is a lot of existing going on: respiration, circulation, digestion, and so on. But how much real living?

Saint John, in his gospel, is a master at telling stories of Jesus in a way that invites us to deeper meaning. The words and symbols don't only tell us something that happened, but tell us what it can mean for us, what can happen to us. We've seen this already in the passages about the woman at the well, or the man born blind. These are readings that are used especially for catechumens, those who are preparing for baptism. They are written as personal encounters that can help the catechumens discern what is happening in their own lives.

> *Now a certain man was ill, Lazarus of Bethany, the village of Mary and her sister Martha. Mary was the one who anointed the Lord with perfume and wiped his feet with her hair; her brother Lazarus was ill. So the sisters sent a message to Jesus, "Lord, he whom you love is ill." But when Jesus heard it, he said, "This illness does not lead to death; rather it is for God's glory, so that the Son*

of God may be glorified through it." Accordingly, though
Jesus loved Martha and her sister and Lazarus, after
having heard that Lazarus was ill, he stayed two days
longer in the place where he was.

Then after this he said to the disciples, "Let us go to
Judea again." (John 11:1-7)

Another one of those stories traditionally used to in-
struct the catechumens is the raising of Lazarus. In the
story of the woman at the well, the dominant image or
code that Jesus uses to speak to her is water. With the
man born blind, the image is light. Now with Lazarus,
Martha, and Mary, the image will be life itself.

When Jesus arrived, he found that Lazarus had already
been in the tomb four days. Now Bethany was near
Jerusalem, some two miles away, and many of the Jews
had come to Martha and Mary to console them about
their brother. When Martha heard that Jesus was coming,
she went and met him, while Mary stayed at home.
Martha said to Jesus, "Lord, if you had been here, my
brother would not have died. But even now I know that
God will give you whatever you ask of him." Jesus said to
her, "Your brother will rise again." Martha said to him,
"I know that he will rise again in the resurrection on the
last day." Jesus said to her, "I am the resurrection and the
life. Those who believe in me, even though they die, will
live, and everyone who lives and believes in me will never
die. Do you believe this?" She said to him, "Yes, Lord,

*I believe that you are the Messiah, the Son of God, the one
coming into the world."...*

*When Mary came where Jesus was and saw him,
she knelt at his feet and said to him, "Lord, if you had
been here, my brother would not have died." When Jesus
saw her weeping, and the Jews who came with her also
weeping, he was greatly disturbed in spirit and deeply
moved. He said, "Where have you laid him?" They said
to him, "Lord, come and see." (John 11:17-27, 32-34)*

The catechumens are invited to make connections between their stories and the story in the Scriptures. Can
we do the same? Do we know what it is like to be Martha
or Mary sitting beside a tomb, waiting, weeping, hoping? We don't understand why the Lord delays; why
we don't receive answers to all our questions or solu-
tions to all our problems in a hurry. We may feel abandoned. We don't understand why it takes so long for us
to learn from our experiences and change our story for
the better. But at the same time, there is the spark of faith
within, ready to trust in something greater than
ourselves.

*Jesus began to weep. So the Jews said, "See how he loved
him!" But some of them said, "Could not he who opened
the eyes of the blind man have kept this man from dying?"
Then Jesus, again greatly disturbed, came to the tomb.
It was a cave, and a stone was lying against it. Jesus said,
"Take away the stone." Martha, the sister of the dead*

> man, said to him, "Lord, already there is a stench because
> he has been dead four days." Jesus said to her, "Did I not
> tell you that if you believed, you would see the glory of
> God?" So they took away the stone. And Jesus looked
> upward and said, "Father, I thank you for having heard
> me. I knew that you always hear me, but I have said this
> for the sake of the crowd standing here, so that they may
> believe that you sent me." When he had said this, he cried
> with a loud voice, "Lazarus, come out!" The dead man
> came out, his hands and feet bound with strips of cloth,
> and his face wrapped in a cloth. Jesus said to them,
> "Unbind him, and let him go." (John 11:35-44)

Do we know what it is like to be Lazarus? Does humanity know? Here's someone who is bound up in cloth, his hands and feet tied with cords. As with the customs of the day, two stones cover his eyes, his mouth is gagged with cloth. He is buried in a cave with a huge stone rolled across the opening. Do we know what it is like to be this helpless? To be vulnerable, frustrated, bound and gagged, at a loss? The name Lazarus means "God is my help." Are we aware of our need and God's power to help?

Are we ever, like Martha, afraid to let Jesus into these tombs? There is a stench. Some things we don't want disturbed. We're not ready for change. We're not ready to roll away the stone and discover what God wants to do with us. But his words beckon us: *"Take away the stone."* This is why he came—to unbind us.

Will we let God help? Jesus wants to encounter us as he did these others in the gospel stories. He wants to meet us in our lives, in our story. He wants to meet us in the big things and the little things, the momentous times and the ordinary times of our life. But we must crack that code, make the connections. Then we'll know what it means not just to exist, or to survive. We'll know what it means to really live.

$\sim$

Beyond

Now among those who went up to worship at the festival were some Greeks. They came to Philip, who was from Bethsaida in Galilee, and said to him, "Sir, we wish to see Jesus." Philip went and told Andrew; then Andrew and Philip went and told Jesus. Jesus answered them, "The hour has come for the Son of Man to be glorified. Very truly, I tell you, unless a grain of wheat falls into the earth and dies, it remains just a single grain; but if it dies, it bears much fruit. Those who love their life lose it, and those who hate their life in this world will keep it for eternal life. Whoever serves me must follow me, and where I am, there will my servant be also. Whoever serves me, the Father will honor." (John 12:20-26)

There's a tradition found in both eastern and western spiritual traditions: the tradition of the spiritual "master" or teacher. We can think of the Bodhisattva in Buddhism, the Hasidic sage, the Sufi master, or the Christian mystic. This is someone who has been on the journey for a long time, someone who has connected with the divine, someone with transcendent wisdom. People notice this and seek the master out in hopes of finding that connection in their own lives. In speaking with some college students once, I drove this point home by citing Obi-Wan Kenobi, which definitely registered from their own "tradition."

Now the spiritual masters sometimes speak in strange ways. This is because they are speaking of things beyond us. They must speak in parables, stories, riddles. They use paradoxes, signs, symbolic actions, and poetry. Oftentimes this is frustrating for those who do not yet fully understand.

There is a story from the east of a disciple who complains to the spiritual teacher: "Master, why do you not speak plainly to us? Why do you tell us these stories and then not explain their meaning?" The master replies: "How would you like it if I offered you an apple, and then said, 'Here, let me chew it for you first?'"

We must do our part. Words alone will not bring us where we want to be. Explanations aren't enough. It's about letting reality in—and letting that reality transform us. With all their diversity, this is something all the sages agree on: Life is a spiritual quest, and learning to live well involves connecting to a reality beyond us. They're all about the spiritual quest. But it's a personal journey, and only we can take it. No one can do it for us, not even the master. The spiritual master just points the way.

Jesus uses the tradition of the spiritual master. He's more than that: he is the way, and he is food for the journey. But he takes on that role for his disciples. He takes on that role in the short passage above.

Some Greeks come to the disciples Philip and Andrew and say, "We wish to see Jesus." They want to meet him and connect with him. They've heard about his signs, his stories, and the effect they are having on people. They know that a true master is among them, someone connected with God, with the spirit within. They want that in their own lives, that connection with the spirit.

And, Jesus, like a good spiritual master, probably frustrates them. He offers no explanations, no easy answers. He offers images, signs, paradoxes. Why? He's pointing them to something, to that spiritual path. "Chew on this," he's saying.

Jesus gives them a couple of good apples here. *"Unless a grain of wheat falls into the earth and dies, it remains just a single grain; but if it dies, it bears much fruit."* What are these words pointing us to? What path are they inviting us on?

We don't just die once. We die all our lives. We let go all our lives. Sometimes it's a stage of life we must let go of. Sometimes it is a set of ideas, ways of thinking about the world or about ourselves, that must die. Or maybe we have to let go of behaviors, old ways of doing things that aren't working anymore. Sometimes it's people to whom we must say goodbye. Maybe we're ready to send them off on their own, like a parent sending their child off on another phase of life. At other times, it feels like they are being torn away from us.

But it's not just about letting go. It's letting go in order to embrace something new. We let go of one stage in life in order to fully embrace another and the challenges it brings. We let go of old ideas and ways of doing things in order to grow, to become wiser, to embrace a new vision of life. We let go of people in order to embrace others in a new way, with a new freedom and love that we didn't know before.

Finally, through those seeds, we come to understand the meaning of letting go, the meaning of dying and rising. And at some point, hopefully when life has matured and ripened, it's life itself that we must let go of in order to grow, to love, to live.

It's about being on that spiritual path. We want to connect with a deeper kind of life. We want to be aware of the dying and rising rather than fight it, as so many do. We give ourselves over to that dying, that letting go, and see the spiritual fruit that rises. We follow the Lord into death so as to rise with him, both now and later.

Another apple, another paradox: *"Those who love their life lose it, and those who hate their life in this world will keep it for eternal life."* We must chew on this. What could it mean? What could it be pointing to?

Are we supposed to be self-loathing? Are we supposed to hate the world? That obviously wouldn't have much in common with everything our faith teaches us about how precious life and creation is, or how we are called to honor, celebrate, and protect it. To dishonor the world would be to dishonor the Creator who made it good. To dishonor life would be to insult the author of life.

Again, Jesus, as a good spiritual master, calls us to see beyond the words. We must see beyond this world in order to live well in this world—because there's a way of living in this world in which we don't see beyond it. There's a way of living in which we're caught up only in what this world says is important: the attitudes, the fears, the attachments, the toys, the tributes, the easy ways out.

We could have everything this world says is important and still be miserable. We could have everything, and it would do us no good. We can live our life in a way that wastes our life. Or we could see beyond this world and discover its meaning. We can build our lives on eternal values and learn to live well. We can "lose" our life, one kind of life, and find a truer, fuller life.

> *"Now my soul is troubled. And what should I say—*
> *'Father, save me from this hour'? No, it is for this reason*
> *that I have come to this hour. Father, glorify your name."*
> *Then a voice came from heaven, "I have glorified it, and*
> *I will glorify it again." The crowd standing there heard it*
> *and said that it was thunder. Others said, "An angel has*
> *spoken to him." Jesus answered, "This voice has come for*
> *your sake, not for mine. Now is the judgment of this*
> *world; now the ruler of this world will be driven out.*
> *And I, when I am lifted up from the earth, will draw all*

people to myself." He said this to indicate the kind of death he was to die. (John 12:27-33)

A voice from heaven is heard, yet the bystanders in the crowd say it's only thunder. They hear something, but they can't tell what it is. Perhaps they haven't been on the path long enough. Perhaps they haven't chewed enough on the paradoxes of life. The spiritual path takes time, understanding, and commitment. The question for us is: will we be a bystander or a disciple? Will we be a dabbler or a Jedi knight?

Jesus said: *"Whoever serves me must follow me."* The disciple is the one who commits to walking the spiritual path. That path runs through our work and study, personal life, family life, community, prayer, and service. Can we hear Jesus saying: *"Follow me"*?

When we're on that path, open to the Lord's guidance, stretching and learning, letting go and embracing, then the same thing may happen to us that happened to Philip and Andrew. Others will notice and say: "We wish to see Jesus. We want to connect with him, too. We want to learn what you've learned and see what you've seen. We want to see beyond."

And we'll have something to share. We'll be able to build up others, and encourage them, and point the way to Jesus, who gives us nourishment for the journey.

~

Second Chances

Early in the morning he came again to the temple. All the people came to him and he sat down and began to teach them. The scribes and the Pharisees brought a woman who had been caught in adultery; and making her stand before all of them, they said to him, "Teacher, this woman was caught in the very act of committing adultery. Now in the law Moses commanded us to stone such women. Now what do you say?" They said this to test him, so that they might have some charge to bring against him. Jesus bent down and wrote with his finger on the ground. (John 8:2-6)

I once attended a wedding in which the minister pointed to an elderly couple in the congregation. They were celebrating their fiftieth wedding anniversary that same day. So the minister tried to draw a connection between them and the newly married couple. During his homily, he said to the older couple: "Fifty years! If you were giving the sermon today, I'm sure you'd tell us it's been fifty years of nothing but smooth sailing!" Everybody in the church laughed on cue. Everybody knows that no one gets through a journey like that together without storms, without lots of challenges.

In fact, knowing some of the strains the couple had to deal with in life and their resilience, someone at the reception asked, "How do they do it?" Another answered: "They believe in a God of second chances."

I don't know where that expression comes from, but most of us have heard it and can certainly relate to it.

We have a God of second chances, and we know we need them. How have you experienced that need? A relationship goes sour; a deal falls through; a child breaks your heart; a tragic disappointment; a deep personal failure. And we ask: How can I get up again after this? Should I even try?

We have a God of second chances. Thank God for that. But how are we at *giving* second chances?

In the passage above, the scribes and Pharisees, the elders of the people, make this woman stand before them and try to use her to critique and attack Jesus. Where is the adulterous man? If they were caught in the act, he must have been around, too. But she is the useful target. They surround her, pointing their fingers.

When we're in the middle of the crowd and others are pointing fingers at us, we suddenly understand ambiguity. We know how complicated life can be. We hope for compassion, for second chances. But when we're in that crowd, that outer circle, how easy it is to point fingers. How quick we are to label, to write people off, to use them, to cling to anger, to blame and scapegoat.

That's a common mechanism in human societies: to scapegoat. We heap all the blame on someone else. We do it to protect ourselves; we do it to feel superior. It's done to individuals. It's done to groups. It's done to the church. We're all good at it.

> *When they kept on questioning him, he straightened up and said to them, "Let anyone among you who is without sin be the first to throw a stone at her." And once again he*

bent down and wrote on the ground. When they heard it,
they went away, one by one, beginning with the elders;
and Jesus was left alone with the woman standing before
him. Jesus straightened up and said to her, "Woman,
where are they? Has no one condemned you?" She said,
"No one, sir." And Jesus said, "Neither do I condemn you.
Go your way, and from now on do not sin again."
(John 8:7-11)

In his gospel, St. John employs interesting details that
seem to come out of nowhere, leaving it up to us to
interpret. Jesus writes on the ground twice in this episode, but we're not told what he writes down. That's left
to our imagination. One thing this tells us, though, is that
Jesus is not participating in the scapegoating. He isn't
putting this person on display or pointing fingers.

People have always wondered, though, about what
Jesus may be writing on the ground. I've heard that one
saint imagined that Jesus first wrote the woman's sins
on the ground, as if to say: Yes, I know who you are.
There is no need to pretend or to hide. But the second
time he wrote down all the sins of those in the crowd
who wanted to condemn her: greed, hatred, stealing,
deceiving, killing.

What room is there for pointing fingers when we all
need second chances? Or third, or fourth? Who can
condemn?

Our beliefs, our moral teachings set a high standard.
They call us to be more than we are. But they are never
a condemnation. They are an invitation. They are an

invitation to the fullness of life. Jesus says to the woman that she is not condemned. She is free to go in peace, and to live now without sin.

"Second chances" don't mean getting off easy. It's not like having a good PR firm behind you to come up with a strategy to rehabilitate your image, as we see so often with public figures. Our faith understands responsibility and justice. It doesn't avoid the consequences of our actions. We learn the wisdom of God's ways in practice.

But our faith gets us to ask deeper questions. There are "religions of the law" that say: here are the rules. Follow them or don't, you'll get what you deserve. It's as easy as that. Christianity is different. It asks: How do people change? What are the principles of our inner transformation? At the heart of our faith is a unique understanding of God's mercy and compassion. At the heart of our way of life is the understanding that the law cannot save us. For us, it is not enough to follow a law. We follow a person who has shown us the way to God. We must understand God's way from within, love it from within, embrace it in freedom.

This transformation comes from having an experience. There are moments in our lives when we cannot pretend, when we cannot blame others, when we come "as we are." These moments can be breakthrough experiences in life, times when we see things as they truly are—and see ourselves as we truly are. And we want something new. We want to find that inner power to leave the past behind and to strive for a new goal: God's goal for us. The woman in the gospel story had this experience through Jesus.

It's because we have an experience of God's justice, God's love, and God's wisdom that we can become just, loving, and wise. This is because only love heals, only God's mercy saves. Our God is a God of second chances. Thank God that, because of Jesus, we can get up again and live again his gift of life.

~

The Gate

See, I have set before you today life and prosperity, death and adversity. If you obey the commandments of the LORD your God that I am commanding you today, by loving the LORD your God, walking in his ways, and observing his commandments, decrees, and ordinances, then you shall live and become numerous, and the LORD your God will bless you in the land that you are entering to possess. But if your heart turns away and you do not hear, but are led astray to bow down to other gods and serve them, I declare to you today that you shall perish; you shall not live long in the land that you are crossing the Jordan to enter and possess. I call heaven and earth to witness against you today that I have set before you life

> *and death, blessings and curses. Choose life so that you*
> *and your descendants may live, loving the LORD your*
> *God, obeying him, and holding fast to him; for that*
> *means life to you and length of days, so that you may live*
> *in the land that the LORD swore to give to your ancestors,*
> *to Abraham, to Isaac, and to Jacob. (Deuteronomy*
> *30:15-20)*

We are presented with a harsh, sharp dichotomy in this reading. We tend to like nuance. We accept how complicated life can be and appreciate fine distinctions. How often people are hurt and crushed when we fail to embrace and understand their complexity. Yet there is no room for compromise or cooperation with evil in this. We've spoken amply of our call to purify our motives and embark on a radical journey toward God. In this reading we are reminded of the stakes involved in such a journey.

Moses has brought the people of Israel to the edge of the promised land. He must leave them with words that will guide them through every challenge to come, words that will summarize their life's mission. A new land stretches out before them with myriad possibilities. He presents them with a choice that sums up every small decision they will have to make, every difficult calculation, every nuanced distinction. In the end, will they choose death or life? It's their decision to make. God has left them free to do so. And Moses leaves them with the words that will echo in their memory forever: Choose life!

> *"Very truly, I tell you, anyone who does not enter the sheepfold by the gate but climbs in by another way is a thief and a bandit. The one who enters by the gate is the shepherd of the sheep. The gatekeeper opens the gate for him, and the sheep hear his voice. He calls his own sheep by name and leads them out. When he has brought out all his own, he goes ahead of them, and the sheep follow him because they know his voice. They will not follow a stranger, but they will run from him because they do not know the voice of strangers." Jesus used this figure of speech with them, but they did not understand what he was saying to them.*
>
> *So again Jesus said to them, "Very truly, I tell you, I am the gate for the sheep. All who came before me are thieves and bandits; but the sheep did not listen to them. I am the gate. Whoever enters by me will be saved, and will come in and go out and find pasture. The thief comes only to steal and kill and destroy. I came that they may have life, and have it abundantly." (John 10:1-10)*

In St. John's gospel, Jesus also makes some sharp distinctions. As we've seen, St. John spends a lot of time on the discourse between Jesus and those who oppose his work. There are forces of darkness and of light, forces that lead people to destruction, and those that lead them to safety. Here, too, Jesus is reminding his followers that they have the freedom to choose. All of life is spread out before them, with its myriad possibilities. Will they follow the voice of the shepherd? Will they seek the gate that leads to good pastures? Will they find the abundant life that they yearn for?

The image of the gate offers a vision of both safety and freedom. The gate doesn't lock behind us. We can come in and go out. We enter to renew our awareness and listen to the voice of wisdom. We leave to fulfill our mission. It is a threshold to choosing. Again, he leaves it to us.

I wonder if sometimes we fail to realize how powerful our choices are. These include the little decisions, as well as the great ones. The communities we are a part of are like living organisms. The effects of our attitudes and actions ripple through to others both near and far. How one treats one's spouse or one's child may affect their lives for decades to come. The attitude that governs the way we act in the office or the classroom may shift our local culture in a positive or negative direction.

I remember working in an office where a leadership void allowed bad behavior from one employee to go unchecked. Soon relationships among the entire work team began to suffer. The whole organism began to disintegrate. People became less productive, and many left the organization. It was as if the flock had no voice to follow, no gate from which to come in and go out.

> *"I am the good shepherd. The good shepherd lays down his life for the sheep. The hired hand, who is not the shepherd*

*and does not own the sheep, sees the wolf coming and
leaves the sheep and runs away—and the wolf snatches
them and scatters them. The hired hand runs away
because a hired hand does not care for the sheep. I am the
good shepherd. I know my own and my own know me,
just as the Father knows me and I know the Father.
And I lay down my life for the sheep." (John 10:11-15)*

Jesus made decisions that affected his disciples and others, decisions that helped to form their culture. He decided to approach the Samaritan woman at the well, even though doing so violated social and religious taboos. He chose to heal the man born blind on the Sabbath, even though this would disturb his opponents. He waited four days before going to the home of Martha and Mary in Bethany, so that God's glory could be revealed in that place. Each of his decisions, even when difficult, was a choice for life. Each has rippled through time and continues to affect the world.

Each small choice in Jesus' life was an enactment of his great choice for life. He remained faithful to the covenant, to his Father's will for the healing of humanity. He laid down his life for those he loved.

The Lord has given us both safety and freedom. He is the gate. He is the shepherd. He has set before us the myriad possibilities of life. Now we must choose. Every day, in little ways and big, we choose.

~

Witness

Nebuchadnezzar said to them, "Is it true, O Shadrach,
Meshach, and Abednego, that you do not serve my gods
and you do not worship the golden statue that I have set
up? Now if you are ready when you hear the sound of the
horn, pipe, lyre, trigon, harp, drum, and entire musical
ensemble to fall down and worship the statue that I have
made, well and good. But if you do not worship, you shall
immediately be thrown into a furnace of blazing fire, and
who is the god that will deliver you out of my hands?"

Shadrach, Meshach, and Abednego answered the king,
"O Nebuchadnezzar, we have no need to present a defense
to you in this matter. If our God whom we serve is able to
deliver us from the furnace of blazing fire and out of your
hand, O king, let him deliver us. But if not, be it known
to you, O king, that we will not serve your gods and we
will not worship the golden statue that you have set up."
(Daniel 3:14-18)

Nebuchadnezzar was the king of Babylon, the great-
est political and military power in the world. When
he asks, *"Who is the god who can deliver you out of my*
hands?"—it was no idle boast. He made the rules everyone followed. Shadrach, Meshach, and Abednego were
not simpletons. They worked under the king as civil
administrators and understood the consequences of
their actions. They had no clear expectation of deliverance from their situation. Yet they came to the conclu-

sion that they could not deny their God. Whether God chose to save them or not, they could not deny the truth of their existence. They could only witness to that truth.

> *Then Nebuchadnezzar was so filled with rage against Shadrach, Meshach, and Abednego that his face was distorted. He ordered the furnace heated up seven times more than was customary, and ordered some of the strongest guards in his army to bind Shadrach, Meshach, and Abednego and to throw them into the furnace of blazing fire. So the men were bound, still wearing their tunics, their trousers, their hats, and their other garments, and they were thrown into the furnace of blazing fire. Because the king's command was urgent and the furnace was so overheated, the raging flames killed the men who lifted Shadrach, Meshach, and Abednego. But the three men, Shadrach, Meshach, and Abednego, fell down, bound, into the furnace of blazing fire.*
>
> *Then King Nebuchadnezzar was astonished and rose up quickly. He said to his counselors, "Was it not three men that we threw bound into the fire?" They answered the king, "True, O king." He replied, "But I see four men unbound, walking in the middle of the fire, and they are not hurt; and the fourth has the appearance of a god." Nebuchadnezzar then approached the door of the furnace of blazing fire and said, "Shadrach, Meshach, and Abednego, servants of the Most High God, come out! Come here!" So Shadrach, Meshach, and Abednego came out from the fire. And the satraps, the prefects, the*

> *governors, and the king's counselors gathered together and*
> *saw that the fire had not had any power over the bodies of*
> *those men; the hair of their heads was not singed, their*
> *tunics were not harmed, and not even the smell of fire*
> *came from them. Nebuchadnezzar said, "Blessed be the*
> *God of Shadrach, Meshach, and Abednego, who has sent*
> *his angel and delivered his servants who trusted in him.*
> *They disobeyed the king's command and yielded up their*
> *bodies rather than serve and worship any god except their*
> *own God." (Daniel 3:19-28)*

The book of Daniel was actually written centuries after the Babylonian exile. Most likely this story was written down to console and strengthen the chosen people as they endured a different persecution, under the Hellenists. The people could see their own plight in the heroes of old and considered how they could hold on to their faith. This is a story that can be told and understood in many different times, cultures, and contexts.

It is more than a story of courage. It is a story about truth and witnessing to truth. Truth endures fiery furnaces and prison walls. It surpasses the power of kings and, in the end, can even overcome their hardened hearts. Truth surpasses any power that is brought against it.

> *Then Jesus said to the Jews who had believed in him,*
> *"If you continue in my word, you are truly my disciples;*
> *and you will know the truth, and the truth will make*
> *you free." They answered him, "We are descendants of*

Abraham and have never been slaves to anyone. What do you mean by saying, 'You will be made free'?"

Jesus answered them, "Very truly, I tell you, everyone who commits sin is a slave to sin. The slave does not have a permanent place in the household; the son has a place there forever. So if the Son makes you free, you will be free indeed." (John 8:31-36)

Jesus sees discipleship, truth, and freedom all tied together. *"Continue in my word,"* he says, and you will know a freedom that goes beyond what lineage, citizenship, kings, or constitutions can give. This is freedom within. This is freedom from sin and death. It comes from God, and we must choose it. We can choose to be slaves of sin, or disciples of truth and freedom.

What will it mean for us to witness to the truth? This is not a false kind of witnessing that relies on external performances or doctrinal debates. It does not offer us security or applause. This is about living in the truth.

God is Truth with a capital "T." When we say that the Bible or church teachings are "true," we do not mean they are God. God is always more. God's truth is transcendent. Revealed teachings are true in that they point us toward God, toward Truth. When we drop the falsehoods and illusions that keep us from the life that God created us for, we witness to the truth.

We witness to truth when we see and understand the true value of things in light of their Creator. We witness to truth when the honors, threats, or pressures of the world have no hold over us. We witness to truth when we choose to follow the path of integrity when there are no rewards.

When we live from the truth of our existence, the truth that God has written in our hearts, we will be living in freedom. Our words and actions will extend from the truest part of ourselves. We will respond to the situations of our lives listening for God's word, choosing his path. We will be witnesses.

~

Faithful

When Abram was ninety-nine years old, the LORD appeared to Abram, and said to him, "I am God Almighty; walk before me, and be blameless. And I will make my covenant between me and you, and will make you exceedingly numerous." Then Abram fell on his face; and God said to him, "As for me, this is my covenant with you: You shall be the ancestor of a multitude of nations. No longer shall your name be Abram, but your name shall be Abraham; for I have made you the ancestor of a multitude of nations. I will make you exceedingly fruitful; and I will make nations of you, and kings shall come from you. I will establish my covenant between me and you, and your offspring after you throughout their generations, for an everlasting covenant, to be God to you and to your offspring after you. . . .

As for Sarai your wife, you shall not call her Sarai,
but Sarah shall be her name. I will bless her, and
moreover I will give you a son by her. I will bless her,
and she shall give rise to nations; kings of peoples shall
come from her." (Genesis 17:1-7, 15-16)

The "catechumenate" is the ancient name for the process of discernment and formation that adults undertake when they feel called to be baptized into the church. Those who prepare for baptism, the "catechumens," spend time studying the Scriptures, applying them to their own experiences, and listening to God's call in their lives. They experience what it means to live and serve with the community. They open themselves to a deeper journey with Jesus. Many are baptized on the evening vigil service that ushers in Easter. Then, in the sacrament of confirmation, they are anointed with oil, hands are laid on them, and they are prayed over, asking God to send the Holy Spirit upon them, giving them gifts to live the Christian life.

Often they will be invited to take a new name, a "confirmation name," if they wish. This recalls times in the Scriptures when people were given new names to indicate how the divine activity in their lives changed them. They were so touched by God's power, their growth was so great, that they took on a new mission. A sign of this was a new name. A great example of this in the New Testament is the changing of Simon's name to "Cephas" (or Peter in Greek), meaning "rock."

But this special way of naming originates, as the passage above shows, in God's initiation of the covenant with the chosen people. Abram becomes "Abraham," and Sarai becomes "Sarah." They are the first to be welcomed into a new "covenant," a unique relationship with God—and this will affect all those coming after them. Their offspring will be part of that covenant.

Now because we are human, this covenant, like all our relationships, will have its ups and downs. Sometimes humans will stumble in their relationship with God. They are weak; they are confused at times. But God is faithful to that covenant. Sometimes we feel like turning our backs on the covenant. We are ready to violate its meaning. But God is faithful. Sometimes we pretend not to see its implications. We are afraid of its demands. But God is faithful. In our lack of awareness, our failure to understand, we harm ourselves. We run from the growth and healing that God wants to give us. God remains faithful.

Margaret Edson's play *Wit* tells the story of a college professor, an expert in the poetry of John Donne, who discovers she has ovarian cancer.[9] In the course of her treatment she confronts her choices in life, professional and personal, that led her away from the human connections she desired. The play follows her decline until a visitor, an old mentor, arrives to speak to her of simple truths that she has avoided for so long, and to offer peace. At one point, the mentor recites a few simple lines from a children's book, which at that moment speak more eloquently of God's search for the soul than the abstract metaphysical poetry they have dissected for years. The scene elicits what much great art tells us in varied forms: Embrace the life you have, and see in it a love that is beyond your own.

How often do we run from the things that can truly make us happy? Have you ever found yourself running from simple truths in pursuit of complicated lies? From those things that we know are healthy for us in favor of those that merely feed our ego? From those people who offer us the best chance at love in favor of self-sufficiency? Have you ever exchanged the most valuable things in life for empty promises?

> *Sing for joy, O heavens, and exult, O earth;*
> *   break forth, O mountains, into singing!*
> *For the LORD has comforted his people,*
> *   and will have compassion on his suffering ones.*
>
> *But Zion said, "The LORD has forsaken me,*
> *   my Lord has forgotten me."*
> *Can a woman forget her nursing child,*
> *   or show no compassion for the child of her womb?*
> *Even these may forget,*
> *   yet I will not forget you.*
> *See, I have inscribed you on the palms of my hands;*
> *   your walls are continually before me.*
> *Your builders outdo your destroyers,*
> *   and those who laid you waste go away from you.*
> *   (Isaiah 49:13-17)*

This is the message of the prophets: Return to the Lord, the faithful one. You will find yourself again in the covenant at the heart of your creation and at the heart of your redemption. God is so faithful to that covenant, to the realization of our healing, that in the fullness of time God seals it in flesh and blood. God comes to us in person to fulfill that covenant, to embrace us, and to welcome us into the new covenant that Jesus brings.

> *"Your ancestor Abraham rejoiced that he would see my day; he saw it and was glad." Then the Jews said to him, "You are not yet fifty years old, and have you seen Abraham?" Jesus said to them, "Very truly, I tell you, before Abraham was, I am." So they picked up stones to throw at him, but Jesus hid himself and went out of the temple. (John 8:56-59)*

Fidelity to the covenant comes with no promise of an easy path. Stones of confusion, misunderstanding, or fear may fly.

At a certain point, catechumens enter a more intense phase of their preparation for baptism. In public prayers called the "scrutinies," they lay themselves bare, asking God to work in them, to reveal their faults, overcome their fears, to bring them out of darkness and into the light. In doing so, they serve as a reminder for the rest of us. We need to remember to value what is most important in life. We need to reject complicated lies, empty promises, and self-sufficiency. We need to recall what the Lord has shown us again and again: that no matter how often we stumble or fall away, no matter how often we run from our own good, God will never forget us. Our God, who is faithful to the covenant, will rush to our aid.

~

The Vine

"I am the true vine, and my Father is the vinegrower. He removes every branch in me that bears no fruit. Every branch that bears fruit he prunes to make it bear more fruit. You have already been cleansed by the word that I have spoken to you. Abide in me as I abide in you. Just as the branch cannot bear fruit by itself unless it abides in the vine, neither can you unless you abide in me. I am the vine, you are the branches. Those who abide in me and I in them bear much fruit, because apart from me you can do nothing. Whoever does not abide in me is thrown away like a branch and withers; such branches are gathered, thrown into the fire, and burned. If you abide in me, and my words abide in you, ask for whatever you wish, and it will be done for you. My Father is glorified by this, that you bear much fruit and become my disciples."
(John 15:1-8)

Saint John, in his depiction of the Last Supper, the last meal that Jesus had with his disciples, presents a lengthy discourse from Jesus. In some ways it is a long farewell address. It shows us what was on Jesus' mind as he prepared for what he knew was coming. He speaks to them of service, of staying strong, of the coming Spirit that will continue to teach them. He prays for their unity. And there is a passage in which he focuses on their union with him, where he uses the image of a vine and its branches.

There are ways in which the parts of a plant—roots, stalk, and fruit—are different, distinct. And there are ways in which they are all one. The life flow is connected; the plant is one. Here we find Jesus' understanding of our mystical union with the divine.

The branch bears fruit when it "abides" in the vine. Life flows through it. How might we apply this image to our own experience? Has our openness to the Lord's life in us born fruit? Spiritual practices like prayer, fasting, study, almsgiving—these are not merely external acts or ends in themselves, but they are ways of opening ourselves to God's action, God's life flowing through us. They are ways the vinegrower can "prune" us so that we may be more fruitful.

What has been your experience of prayer? Has it made you more aware of the abiding presence of God with you? Have times of fasting made you more aware of the needs of the world around you? Have both resulted in concrete actions in service and love? Has there been listening, sharing, connecting, peacemaking, respecting, doing?

How will the experience of walking this road affect your future? How will you incorporate new insights and patterns? Will there be ongoing action, ongoing community, ongoing "abiding"?

> *As the Father has loved me, so I have loved you; abide in my love. If you keep my commandments, you will abide in my love, just as I have kept my Father's commandments and abide in his love. I have said these things to you so that my joy may be in you, and that your joy may be complete.*
>
> *This is my commandment, that you love one another as I have loved you. No one has greater love than this, to lay down one's life for one's friends. You are my friends if you do what I command you. I do not call you servants any longer, because the servant does not know what the master is doing; but I have called you friends, because I have made known to you everything that I have heard from my Father. You did not choose me but I chose you. And I appointed you to go and bear fruit, fruit that will last, so that the Father will give you whatever you ask him in my name. I am giving you these commands so that you may love one another. (John 15:9-17)*

Here is another unique feature of our Christian faith. For those who abide in Christ, there is a participation in the divine life itself. God takes us up into the life and love of the Trinity. *"As the Father has loved me, so I have loved you."* Those who come to know the love that Jesus shows by laying down his life are no longer mere "servants" of God. They are "friends" of God. We are raised to new intimacy with the author of life. We are empowered to walk the divine path, to live the divine commandments—all because we have been called to know and abide in his love.

Jesus is the Lord, the one sent to share our lives and to lay down his life for our sake, for our salvation. We are about to enter the highpoint of this revelation of God to us. The road has taken us to the gates of Jerusalem. In some way, we accompany Jesus on this path to where he fulfills his mission. We can only believe in all this— that Jesus is Lord, that he is God's love in person, sent to save us—when we can believe in a God who loves us that much.

SIX

The City

Well and good if all things change, O Lord God, provided I am rooted in You.

—St. John of the Cross,
The Sayings of Light and Love

Jerusalem

*When they had come near Jerusalem and had reached
Bethphage, at the Mount of Olives, Jesus sent two
disciples, saying to them, "Go into the village ahead of
you, and immediately you will find a donkey tied, and a
colt with her; untie them and bring them to me. If anyone
says anything to you, just say this, 'The Lord needs them.'
And he will send them immediately." This took place to
fulfill what had been spoken through the prophet, saying,*

> *"Tell the daughter of Zion,*
> *Look, your king is coming to you,*
> *humble, and mounted on a donkey,*
> *and on a colt, the foal of a donkey."*
> *(Matthew 21:1-5)*

This is the week. This is where it all has been leading.
Jesus decides to enter Jerusalem for the final time, knowing that it is the time of fulfillment for him.

Think of the cities in your life. Think of the places
where human begins gather in all their diversity and
cacophony. Can Jerusalem be very different?

It is a volatile time in Jerusalem. The city is dealing
with its own contradictions and emotions. There are
warring political camps and religious parties. There is
suffering under a hated occupying force and deep hope
for liberation. There are those who are angry and want
to incite trouble. There are those who are afraid and
want safety. Jesus knows, too, that there is hostility

building up towards him. There are people, powerful people, who are offended by his intimacy with God and the freedom it gives him. It would have been easy for him to stay away from the ferment, to avoid the mess.

> *The disciples went and did as Jesus had directed them; they brought the donkey and the colt, and put their cloaks on them, and he sat on them. A very large crowd spread their cloaks on the road, and others cut branches from the trees and spread them on the road. The crowds that went ahead of him and that followed were shouting,*
>
> > *"Hosanna to the Son of David!*
> > > *Blessed is the one who comes in the name of the Lord!*
> > *Hosanna in the highest heaven!"*
>
> *When he entered Jerusalem, the whole city was in turmoil, asking, "Who is this?" The crowds were saying, "This is the prophet Jesus from Nazareth in Galilee." (Matthew 21:6-11)*

Matthew tells us *"the whole city was in turmoil,"* as Jesus entered it. I've heard that the word Matthew uses to describe Jerusalem, which is translated here as "turmoil," is the same word that he will use when Jesus dies on the cross and we are told *"the earth shook"* (Matthew 27:51).

The city "shook" when Jesus entered it. We are being prepared to understand the meaning of this last week in Jesus' life. All creation is feeling the effects of this radical moment in history. The earth shook, the heavens shook, the gates of hell shook. These events are strong enough to shake us, too. They can shake us to our roots. They can open our hearts and change our lives.

This story comes to us from another time, another culture, another city. But it is our story. Can we understand a people who move from singing "hosanna" to shouting "crucify him" in the course of a week? Do we know what it is like to totter between hope and fear in the face of the dangers and unknowns of our lives?

This story works because we were there. Pilate and the Romans stand in for us in their ambivalence and cruelty. The religious authorities stand in for us in their fear and hypocrisy. The disciples and crowds stand in for us in their ignorance, apathy, betrayal, and denial. And because of his mercy and love, Jesus chooses to stand in for us in his innocence and fidelity to God's will. Our healing and liberation begin there.

> *As he was now approaching the path down from the Mount of Olives, the whole multitude of the disciples began to praise God joyfully with a loud voice for all the deeds of power that they had seen, saying,*
>
> > *"Blessed is the king*
> > > *who comes in the name of the Lord!*
> > *Peace in heaven,*
> > > *and glory in the highest heaven!"*

> *Some of the Pharisees in the crowd said to him, "Teacher,*
> *order your disciples to stop." He answered, "I tell you,*
> *if these were silent, the stones would shout out." (Luke*
> *19:37-40)*

Thank God that Jesus didn't stay away from Jerusalem that week. Thank God that he didn't play it safe but chose to walk into the mess of it all. He came to the city armed with nothing but God's intention and love. He came into this world for us, embraced it, and brought the only thing that can save it.

Anointing

What do you think you would do if you knew that you were about to meet your destiny? What would you need in order to face a momentous time in your life? During his final days, Jesus spent time in Bethany, a small village outside Jerusalem and home to his friends, Martha, Mary, and Lazarus.

> *Six days before the Passover Jesus came to Bethany, the*
> *home of Lazarus, whom he had raised from the dead.*
> *There they gave a dinner for him. Martha served, and*
> *Lazarus was one of those at the table with him. Mary*

> took a pound of costly perfume made of pure nard,
> anointed Jesus' feet, and wiped them with her hair.
> The house was filled with the fragrance of the perfume.
> But Judas Iscariot, one of his disciples (the one who was
> about to betray him), said, "Why was this perfume not
> sold for three hundred denarii and the money given to the
> poor?" (He said this not because he cared about the poor,
> but because he was a thief; he kept the common purse and
> used to steal what was put into it.) Jesus said, "Leave her
> alone. She bought it so that she might keep it for the day
> of my burial. You always have the poor with you, but you
> do not always have me." (John 12:1-8)

After Jesus' entrance into Jerusalem, three of the four gospel accounts mention a unique event: an anointing of Jesus at Bethany. Matthew and Mark mention an unnamed woman who anoints Jesus' head with oil. It is depicted as a prophetic act (remember that the word "Christ" means "the anointed one"). In John's gospel, some details differ. The anointing is of Jesus' feet, and the woman is identified as Mary, the sister of Martha and Lazarus. In this case, too, the anointing is a prophetic action anticipating Jesus' sacrifice.

We are told that Mary *"anointed Jesus' feet, and wiped them with her hair."* It's easy to pass over these verses without letting the strangeness of this description affect us. After all, people in that day probably did a lot of things that would sound strange to us. Maybe Mary's action with her hair would have made sense in that culture. We assume John's readers would have understood.

I was surprised, then, when I discovered that some commentators on these verses claim that what Mary did would've seemed just as strange in her day. Perhaps even more so, given that a respectable Jewish woman would not normally appear in public with her hair unbound. If this is the case, then we can let the unusualness of this act hit us with its full force: Mary wiped Jesus' feet with her hair.

And fragrance filled the house. She didn't skimp on the ointment. She used loads of this costly perfumed oil. It would have cost three hundred denarii—three hundred days wages. Judas, despite his motivations, rationally questions this act. Isn't this a wasteful deed in the face of what could have been done with the money? Doesn't it fly in the face of Jesus' concerns for the poor? Isn't it impractical and irresponsible? (In fact, the other gospel accounts depict *all* the disciples as indignant over this extravagance.)

Mary's action in the gospel is extravagant, wasteful—and public. Didn't she realize how foolish she must have looked? Was this a courageous act? Or was her attention so fixed on Jesus that it didn't matter to her what she looked like as she displayed her love and gratitude in a lavish act of devotion?

I remember a time when I was in college and a friend asked me flat out: "So, why pray? I go to church sometimes and wonder what this is for. I could be doing other, more useful and important things. God doesn't need me here. Why pray?" We groped for a while, but a purely rational, measured, convincing argument wasn't there. I knew it was meaningful to pray, that prayer is somehow at the heart of what it means to be human and alive. But this prayer was also wasting precious time. It was wasting time to be with the beloved.

Another college memory: I was enlisted by my room-mate to leave our dorm room in the middle of a cold winter night so I could accompany him on my guitar while he attempted to serenade his girlfriend under her dorm window. His bad singing should have been an embarrassment, but all I remember is the joy on his face. There's no rational argument that makes us delight in giving things away, or giving things up, for those we love.

We are so protective of our time until a friend needs it. We are ready to do things for family members that we wouldn't ordinarily do for ourselves. We can even be impractical, reckless in our devotion to those we love.

Jesus has made his way to Jerusalem, and he will show the foolishness of his love, wasting his own blood in a supreme act of devotion to God and to his friends. It's that devotion that gives meaning to our service to those in need. It's that devotion that fills our work on behalf of the world. It makes our service Christian.

For those who worship in liturgical traditions, "Holy Week"—the week that solemnly recalls the final week in Jesus' life—is a busy time. The most significant and intricate worship services of the year are planned. Pastoral and liturgical ministers rehearse and hurry around to make things ready. It's all done in hopes that the power of the Holy Week liturgies will draw our attention away from our preoccupation with ourselves to the Word we serve, the Lord we celebrate.

We spend hours together in church this week, wasting our time on God and on one another. We sing songs to the Lord, create beautiful things for him, give thanks and rejoice in him. It only makes sense because of love and devotion.

> *"By pouring this ointment on my body she has prepared me for burial. Truly I tell you, wherever this good news is proclaimed in the whole world, what she has done will be told in remembrance of her." (Matthew 26:12-13)*

The story of the anointing at Bethany stakes out a place at the center of our faith. It's the story of a devotion that doesn't count the cost. It's a foolish response to God's foolishness. We allow God to lavish on us the fragrant perfume of his own life. This is what our remembrances, our extravagant liturgies, our prayer is all about, as we turn our full attention to Jesus.

$\sim$

Passion

The Lord GOD has given me
the tongue of a teacher,
that I may know how to sustain
the weary with a word.

Morning by morning he wakens—
  wakens my ear
  to listen as those who are taught.
The Lord GOD has opened my ear,
  and I was not rebellious,
  I did not turn backward.
I gave my back to those who struck me,
  and my cheeks to those who pulled out the beard;
I did not hide my face
  from insult and spitting.
The Lord GOD helps me;
  therefore I have not been disgraced;
therefore I have set my face like flint,
  and I know that I shall not be put to shame;
  he who vindicates me is near. (Isaiah 50:4-8)

The book of the prophet Isaiah has several passages that are known as the "Suffering Servant" songs. They depict the life of a servant of God, a disciple who *"morning by morning"* opens his ears to God's word. This servant accepts his vocation to teach others the message that he has taken to heart, words *"to sustain the weary."* It is a call to bring hope and encouragement to others, to lift hearts to God.

But not everyone accepts the servant's words. There are some who even actively oppose his mission, insulting and beating him. Even in the face of rejection, though, the servant trusts in God's help.

There is no wonder that Christians from the beginning have seen these passages fulfilled in the life of

Jesus, one sent to teach us to hope in God and to live as his children, one who experienced rejection yet remained strong in his commitment to God's will. In fact, Christians see no one other than Jesus who, in his passion, perfectly fulfills this prophecy.

Who has believed what we have heard?
And to whom has the arm of the LORD been revealed?
For he grew up before him like a young plant,
and like a root out of dry ground;
he had no form or majesty that we should look at him,
nothing in his appearance that we should desire him.
He was despised and rejected by others;
a man of suffering and acquainted with infirmity;
and as one from whom others hide their faces
he was despised, and we held him of no account.

Surely he has borne our infirmities
and carried our diseases;
yet we accounted him stricken,
struck down by God, and afflicted.
But he was wounded for our transgressions,
crushed for our iniquities;
upon him was the punishment that made us whole,
and by his bruises we are healed.
All we like sheep have gone astray;
we have all turned to our own way,
and the LORD has laid on him
the iniquity of us all.

He was oppressed, and he was afflicted,
*   yet he did not open his mouth;*
like a lamb that is led to the slaughter,
*   and like a sheep that before its shearers is silent,*
*   so he did not open his mouth.*
By a perversion of justice he was taken away.
*   Who could have imagined his future?*
For he was cut off from the land of the living,
*   stricken for the transgression of my people.*
They made his grave with the wicked
*   and his tomb with the rich,*
although he had done no violence,
*   and there was no deceit in his mouth.*
Yet it was the will of the LORD to crush him with pain.
When you make his life an offering for sin,
*   he shall see his offspring, and shall prolong his days;*
through him the will of the LORD shall prosper.
*   Out of his anguish he shall see light;*
he shall find satisfaction through his knowledge.
*   The righteous one, my servant, shall make many*
*   righteous,*
*   and he shall bear their iniquities.*
Therefore I will allot him a portion with the great,
*   and he shall divide the spoil with the strong;*
because he poured out himself to death,
*   and was numbered with the transgressors;*
yet he bore the sin of many,
*   and made intercession for the transgressors.*
*   (Isaiah 53:1-12)*

We often use the word "passion" to indicate strong feelings. We think of the inner drives of our heart, our deepest desires, moving us to act. Our passion consumes us like a burning fire. But there's more. The Latin root, *passio*, points directly to an experience of suffering. It relates to a surrender—a submitting, a letting go—to something beyond us.

There comes a time when we all "lose control" over life, and we are then confronted with different kinds of choices. Viktor Frankl, the famous Holocaust survivor, became a psychologist and developed what he called "logotherapy." In his book *Man's Search for Meaning*, he tells stories of those who were able to pass through the horrors of the camps and those who were not. Those who maintained meaning endured. Frankl wrote: ". . . everything can be taken from a man but one thing: the last of the human freedoms—to choose one's attitude in any given set of circumstances, to choose one's own way."[10]

When Jesus enters into his "passion," he could have responded as others would have. He could have run, left town, hid. He could have railed against the injustice. He could have, like one of the thieves with whom he was crucified, cursed God. But he chose to do what he always did, to be who he always was. He chose to maintain the truth of his identity and his call. He chose to reach out to those in need, to forgive even from the cross. He chose to love till the end.

Like Jesus, we carry a message in our words and our lives. In the face of rejection, we too can find help in the

Lord's words of encouragement, in his endurance, in his hope. We will all face a passion in our lives, a time of surrender. Jesus once said to Peter:

> *"Very truly, I tell you, when you were younger, you used to fasten your own belt and to go wherever you wished. But when you grow old, you will stretch out your hands, and someone else will fasten a belt around you and take you where you do not wish to go." (John 21:18)*

May we always remember and draw strength from the Lord's passion, the source of our hope.

~

The Door

> *Then Judas Iscariot, who was one of the twelve, went to the chief priests in order to betray him to them. When they heard it, they were greatly pleased, and promised to give him money. So he began to look for an opportunity to betray him.*
>
> *On the first day of Unleavened Bread, when the Passover lamb is sacrificed, his disciples said to him, "Where do you want us to go and make the preparations for you to eat the Passover?" So he sent two of his disciples, saying to them, "Go into the city, and a man carrying a jar of water will meet you; follow him, and wherever he*

enters, say to the owner of the house, 'The Teacher asks, Where is my guest room where I may eat the Passover with my disciples?' He will show you a large room upstairs, furnished and ready. Make preparations for us there." So the disciples set out and went to the city, and found everything as he had told them; and they prepared the Passover meal.

When it was evening, he came with the twelve. And when they had taken their places and were eating, Jesus said, "Truly I tell you, one of you will betray me, one who is eating with me." They began to be distressed and to say to him one after another, "Surely, not I?" He said to them, "It is one of the twelve, one who is dipping bread into the bowl with me. For the Son of Man goes as it is written of him, but woe to that one by whom the Son of Man is betrayed! It would have been better for that one not to have been born." . . .

And Jesus said to them, "You will all become deserters; for it is written,

> *'I will strike the shepherd,
>   and the sheep will be scattered.'*

But after I am raised up, I will go before you to Galilee." Peter said to him, "Even though all become deserters, I will not." Jesus said to him, "Truly I tell you, this day, this very night, before the cock crows twice, you will deny me three times." But he said vehemently, "Even though I must die with you, I will not deny you." And all of them said the same. (Mark 14:10-21, 27-31)

When Jesus approached his final days, the darkest hours of his life, no one made it easier for him: not his own people, nor the Gentiles, nor even his very own, his inner circle, those he taught, healed, and loved. That must have hurt the most. And yet still he chose to serve them, to reach out to them. Even in this distress, there is nothing they can do that can make him love them less.

If only Judas knew this. Imagine what a powerful passage would have been written in the Scriptures. It would have been a source of meditation through the ages. Imagine how the scene would have been depicted in art and music. Imagine Caravaggio's *Repentance of St. Judas*. Imagine the churches built in his honor, the pilgrimages celebrating his return.

It is not an unthinkable scene. Redemption was available to him as it was and is to everyone. A door was open to him. No matter how far one sinks, there is no limit to how far the Lord will go to embrace us and raise us to a new height.

If we are honest with ourselves, we know that we are capable of the same desertion as the first disciples. If we look into ourselves, we see our weakness and willingness to betray what we hold dear. How easy it would be for us to deny the Lord in his need.

But, no matter how low we think we've sunk; no matter how serious we think our sin, or how troubling our questions, or how deep our hurts—there is a door open for us. No matter how bad a mess we've gotten ourselves into, how lost we feel, or how trapped—there is an embrace, a grace that will not forsake us.

Notes

1. Robert Frost, "The Road Not Taken," in *Mountain Interval* (New York: Henry Holt, 1916).

2. David Loxterkamp, "The Road to Compostela: A Doctor Takes Stock," *Commonweal* 131, no. 4 (February 27, 2004): 16–18.

3. Thomas Ryan, ed., *Reclaiming the Body in Christian Spirituality* (Mahwah, NJ: Paulist Press, 2005).

4. Ryan, ed., *Reclaiming the Body*, 53–55.

5. Elisabeth Kübler-Ross, *On Death and Dying: What the Dying Have to Teach Doctors, Nurses, Clergy and Their Own Families*, 50th anniversary ed. (New York: Scribner, 2014).

6. Annie Dillard, *Pilgrim at Tinker Creek* (New York: Harper, 2007).

7. Henri Nouwen, ¡*Gracias!: A Latin American Journal* (Maryknoll, NY: Orbis Books, 1993).

8. Angelo Scarano, *The Prodigal Father* (Collegeville, MN: Liturgical Press, 2014).

9. Margaret Edson, *Wit: A Play* (New York: Farrar, Straus and Giroux, 1999).

10. Viktor E. Frankl, *Man's Search for Meaning* (Boston: Beacon, 2006), 66.

In John's gospel, the risen Lord calls Mary Magdalene by name. That's when she knows he is alive. It begins with an experience that becomes a message.

In our lives, in our experiences, in whatever circumstances we find ourselves in—easy or difficult, joyful or scary—the risen Lord is going to be there to meet us. He wants to begin a new journey with us. The same Spirit who was at work in Jesus wants to work in you. He is calling you by name. He is calling each of us into that new life that resurrection faith brings.

But Mary stood weeping outside the tomb. As she wept,
she bent over to look into the tomb; and she saw two
angels in white, sitting where the body of Jesus had been
lying, one at the head and the other at the feet. They said
to her, "Woman, why are you weeping?" She said to them,
"They have taken away my Lord, and I do not know
where they have laid him." When she had said this, she
turned around and saw Jesus standing there, but she did
not know that it was Jesus. Jesus said to her, "Woman,
why are you weeping? Whom are you looking for?"
Supposing him to be the gardener, she said to him,
"Sir, if you have carried him away, tell me where you
have laid him, and I will take him away." Jesus said to
her, "Mary!" She turned and said to him in Hebrew,
"Rabbouni!" (which means Teacher). Jesus said to her,
"Do not hold on to me, because I have not yet ascended to
the Father. But go to my brothers and say to them, 'I am
ascending to my Father and your Father, to my God and
your God.'" Mary Magdalene went and announced to the
disciples, "I have seen the Lord"; and she told them that
he had said these things to her. (John 20:11-18)

The resurrection appearances were reserved for a small group of disciples (actually, several hundred, according to the Scriptures) at the beginning of Christianity. Yet, as extraordinary as these appearances were, there's a certain ordinariness to them, too. These were not ecstatic, dreamlike, mystical experiences. They were encounters, so human, so real. In them we see the simple joy of recognition.

> *But where sin increased, grace abounded all the more.*
> *(Romans 5:20)*

The door is open for us.

$$\sim$$

The Servant

We've all experienced endings of some kind. We had to leave home, to move to a new place, to say goodbye to something or someone we'd known. Endings are difficult. Especially when we have shared our lives with those we must leave.

Jesus and his disciples shared so much. They shared time together, listened together to stories and teachings, took risks, saw new places, and had new experiences. They worked through crises, reacted to people's pain, and responded to their needs. They shared laughter, insights, prayer, and silence on the roads they travelled together. They shared life. And through it all the disciples resonated with the Spirit and hope that Jesus showed them.

> *Now before the festival of the Passover, Jesus knew that his*
> *hour had come to depart from this world and go to the*
> *Father. Having loved his own who were in the world,*
> *he loved them to the end. The devil had already put it*
> *into the heart of Judas son of Simon Iscariot to betray*

*him. And during supper Jesus, knowing that the Father
had given all things into his hands, and that he had come
from God and was going to God, got up from the table,
took off his outer robe, and tied a towel around himself.
Then he poured water into a basin and began to wash the
disciples' feet and to wipe them with the towel that was
tied around him. He came to Simon Peter, who said to
him, "Lord, are you going to wash my feet?" Jesus
answered, "You do not know now what I am doing,
but later you will understand." Peter said to him,
"You will never wash my feet." Jesus answered, "Unless I
wash you, you have no share with me." Simon Peter said
to him, "Lord, not my feet only but also my hands and
my head!" Jesus said to him, "One who has bathed does
not need to wash, except for the feet, but is entirely clean.
And you are clean, though not all of you." For he knew
who was to betray him; for this reason he said, "Not all of
you are clean."*

*After he had washed their feet, had put on his robe,
and had returned to the table, he said to them, "Do you
know what I have done to you? You call me Teacher and
Lord—and you are right, for that is what I am. So if I,
your Lord and Teacher, have washed your feet, you also
ought to wash one another's feet. For I have set you an
example, that you also should do as I have done to you.
Very truly, I tell you, servants are not greater than their
master, nor are messengers greater than the one who sent
them. If you know these things, you are blessed if you do
them." (John 13:1-17)*

Have you ever been shocked by someone's service? Someone I know, while travelling alone in Europe, found himself in a Greek city, hopelessly lost at a bus station. As much as he tried to make himself understood, no one could help him. One man, who was waiting for his own bus, saw his distress, and decided to spend some time with him. He examined his map, brought him to another platform, and then waited with this stranger till the bus he needed came. The man did all this even though it meant he missed his own bus.

A college student was planning a ski trip with a group of her friends. The three-day weekend they were waiting for finally arrived, but that's when she suddenly came down with a flu and had to cancel going along. Another member of the group who had also been looking forward to the trip, her roommate, decided that she would cancel, too, so that she could stay with her sick friend, make her meals, and go to the drugstore for her in case she needed it.

These might be small, simple things. Yet I heard of them years after they happened. The stories were still being told. The meaning of these acts stayed with those who were served. They meant that much.

After two millennia, we still remember a simple act of service. At the Last Supper with his disciples, Jesus washed their feet. On one level, it is a simple act. It may not be a practice that we relate to well today, since we don't do it in public. But in a desert community at that time, washing feet was like washing hands. As one came in from the dusty roads, it was a welcomed homecoming gesture.

On another level, though, something deeper is going on. We see this in Peter's reaction of shock. Some commentators mention that the act of washing another's feet would not have been a requirement for anyone, even Jewish slaves. However, it could be seen as a sign of devotion performed by a student to the teacher, a disciple to the master. But *never* the other way around.

That's why Peter is shocked. *"You will never wash my feet."* He knows he's the disciple, and that Jesus is breaking the rules. Jesus answers, *"Unless I wash you, you have no share with me."* He's saying: Unless you accept me in this role, you have no part in what I've come to bring.

We've seen already how John calls the miracles in Jesus' ministry "signs." They point to something and provoke questions of meaning. This washing is likewise a sign, a prophetic act that is pointing to the whole mystery of Jesus' life and death. It contains the meaning of his saving actions, his self-emptying. He is inviting his disciples into the meaning of the laying down of his life, into the mystery of salvation.

Jesus is reversing the roles here, not just of teacher and student, but of God and humanity. For St. John, here is the Word made flesh, the Lord of the Universe, getting on his knees for us, humbling himself for us, serving us. That's the shocking reality of God's love in the face of our need. It's only by allowing Jesus to be our servant, accepting him in his role as our savior, that we are saved and come to share God's life.

And there's another part to the mystery. In discovering who Jesus is, and the role he takes on for us, we discover who we are. *"You also should do as I have done to you."* The disciple is the one who accepts Jesus in his role and, in turn, takes on that role in his or her own life for others. By loving and extending ourselves, we participate in Jesus' own life and service. We become one with him.

Imagine being those servants: no longer obsessed with dominating others, no longer consumed with self-serving, no longer thinking only of what's in it for them. Imagine breaking those rules. Imagine being so full of life that it is a joy to extend oneself, to empty oneself.

Imagine the effect of those servants on the world: little things at a bus stop, or big things that transform organizations and systems. Have we shocked anyone with our service? Would anyone think of us in that role? It's in our shocking love for one another that we become "signs," drawing others into the mystery of Jesus' life and salvation.

> *While they were eating, Jesus took a loaf of bread, and after blessing it he broke it, gave it to the disciples, and said, "Take, eat; this is my body." Then he took a cup, and after giving thanks he gave it to them, saying, "Drink from it, all of you; for this is my blood of the covenant, which is poured out for many for the forgiveness of sins. I tell you, I will never again drink of this fruit of the vine until that day when I drink it new with you in my Father's kingdom." (Matthew 26:26-29)*

On that night, that time of ending, of farewell, Jesus takes them to the heart of his mission, and to his own heart. His action with the bread and wine becomes the living sign shared for all ages. It is the gift of his life, his body and blood, extended to us in our own time, our own body and blood. From the earliest writings of the New Testament, the epistles of St. Paul, we see this as already the living tradition of the church:

> *For I received from the Lord what I also handed on to you, that the Lord Jesus on the night when he was betrayed took a loaf of bread, and when he had given thanks, he broke it and said, "This is my body that is for you. Do this in remembrance of me." In the same way he took the cup also, after supper, saying, "This cup is the new covenant in my blood. Do this, as often as you drink it, in remembrance of me." For as often as you eat this bread and drink the cup, you proclaim the Lord's death until he comes. (1 Corinthians 11:23-26)*

On that night, Jesus brought his disciples together, washed their feet, shared the Eucharist, and said, *"Do this in remembrance of me."* We do that. In our churches, we come together, we wash feet, and we share the Eucharist, all in remembrance of him. And God's love makes us one.

~

Last Words

They went to a place called Gethsemane; and he said to his disciples, "Sit here while I pray." He took with him Peter and James and John, and began to be distressed and agitated. And he said to them, "I am deeply grieved, even to death; remain here, and keep awake." And going a little farther, he threw himself on the ground and prayed that, if it were possible, the hour might pass from him. He said, "Abba, Father, for you all things are possible; remove this cup from me; yet, not what I want, but what you want." (Mark 14:32-36)

Now the chief priests and the whole council were looking for false testimony against Jesus so that they might put him to death, but they found none, though many false witnesses came forward. At last two came forward and said, "This fellow said, 'I am able to destroy the temple of God and to build it in three days.'" The high priest stood up and said, "Have you no answer? What is it that they testify against you?" But Jesus was silent. Then the high priest said to him, "I put you under oath before the living God, tell us if you are the Messiah, the Son of God." Jesus said to him, "You have said so. But I tell you,

> *From now on you will see the Son of Man*
>   *seated at the right hand of Power*
>   *and coming on the clouds of heaven."*

Then the high priest tore his clothes and said, "He has blasphemed! Why do we still need witnesses? You have

*now heard his blasphemy. What is your verdict?" They
answered, "He deserves death." Then they spat in his
face and struck him; and some slapped him, saying,
"Prophesy to us, you Messiah! Who is it that struck you?"
(Matthew 26:59-68)*

*Pilate then called together the chief priests, the leaders,
and the people, and said to them, "You brought me this
man as one who was perverting the people; and here
I have examined him in your presence and have not
found this man guilty of any of your charges against him.
Neither has Herod, for he sent him back to us. Indeed,
he has done nothing to deserve death. I will therefore have
him flogged and release him."*

*Then they all shouted out together, "Away with this
fellow! Release Barabbas for us!" (This was a man who
had been put in prison for an insurrection that had taken
place in the city, and for murder.) Pilate, wanting to
release Jesus, addressed them again; but they kept shouting,
"Crucify, crucify him!" A third time he said to them,
"Why, what evil has he done? I have found in him no
ground for the sentence of death; I will therefore have him
flogged and then release him." But they kept urgently
demanding with loud shouts that he should be crucified;
and their voices prevailed. So Pilate gave his verdict that
their demand should be granted. (Luke 23:13-24)*

*Then the soldiers led him into the courtyard of the palace
(that is, the governor's headquarters); and they called
together the whole cohort. And they clothed him in a*

*purple cloak; and after twisting some thorns into a crown,
they put it on him. And they began saluting him,
"Hail, King of the Jews!" They struck his head with a
reed, spat upon him, and knelt down in homage to him.
After mocking him, they stripped him of the purple cloak
and put his own clothes on him. Then they led him out
to crucify him.*

*They compelled a passer-by, who was coming in from
the country, to carry his cross; it was Simon of Cyrene,
the father of Alexander and Rufus. Then they brought
Jesus to the place called Golgotha (which means the place
of a skull). And they offered him wine mixed with myrrh;
but he did not take it. And they crucified him, and
divided his clothes among them, casting lots to decide
what each should take.*

*It was nine o'clock in the morning when they crucified
him. The inscription of the charge against him read,
"The King of the Jews." And with him they crucified two
bandits, one on his right and one on his left. Those who
passed by derided him, shaking their heads and saying,
"Aha! You who would destroy the temple and build it in
three days, save yourself, and come down from the cross!"
In the same way the chief priests, along with the scribes,
were also mocking him among themselves and saying,
"He saved others; he cannot save himself. Let the Messiah,
the King of Israel, come down from the cross now, so that
we may see and believe." Those who were crucified with
him also taunted him.*

*When it was noon, darkness came over the whole land
until three in the afternoon. At three o'clock Jesus cried out*

with a loud voice, *"Eloi, Eloi, lema sabachthani?"* which means, *"My God, my God, why have you forsaken me?"* (Mark 15:16-34)

Then Jesus said, *"Father, forgive them; for they do not know what they are doing."* . . .

One of the criminals who were hanged there kept deriding him and saying, *"Are you not the Messiah? Save yourself and us!"* But the other rebuked him, saying, *"Do you not fear God, since you are under the same sentence of condemnation? And we indeed have been condemned justly, for we are getting what we deserve for our deeds, but this man has done nothing wrong."* Then he said, *"Jesus, remember me when you come into your kingdom."* He replied, *"Truly I tell you, today you will be with me in Paradise."* (Luke 23:34, 39-43)

Meanwhile, standing near the cross of Jesus were his mother, and his mother's sister, Mary the wife of Clopas, and Mary Magdalene. When Jesus saw his mother and the disciple whom he loved standing beside her, he said to his mother, *"Woman, here is your son."* Then he said to the disciple, *"Here is your mother."* And from that hour the disciple took her into his own home.

After this, when Jesus knew that all was now finished, he said (in order to fulfill the scripture), *"I am thirsty."* A jar full of sour wine was standing there. So they put a sponge full of the wine on a branch of hyssop and held it to his mouth. When Jesus had received the wine, he said, *"It is finished."* (John 19:25-30)

Then Jesus, crying with a loud voice, said, "Father, into your hands I commend my spirit." Having said this, he breathed his last. When the centurion saw what had taken place, he praised God and said, "Certainly this man was innocent." And when all the crowds who had gathered there for this spectacle saw what had taken place, they returned home, beating their breasts. But all his acquaintances, including the women who had followed him from Galilee, stood at a distance, watching these things. (Luke 23:46-49)

When evening had come, and since it was the day of Preparation, that is, the day before the sabbath, Joseph of Arimathea, a respected member of the council, who was also himself waiting expectantly for the kingdom of God, went boldly to Pilate and asked for the body of Jesus. . . . Then Joseph bought a linen cloth, and taking down the body, wrapped it in the linen cloth, and laid it in a tomb that had been hewn out of the rock. He then rolled a stone against the door of the tomb. Mary Magdalene and Mary the mother of Joses saw where the body was laid. (Mark 15:42-43, 46-47)

Cross Over

In the beginning when God created the heavens and the earth, the earth was a formless void and darkness covered

> *the face of the deep, while a wind from God swept over the face of the waters. Then God said, "Let there be light"; and there was light. (Genesis 1:1-3)*

In liturgical traditions, the Easter Vigil service, celebrated after sundown on Holy Saturday, is considered the highpoint of the liturgical year. As Sunday is to the week, this night is to the year. We wait in vigil prayer, anticipating God's great act of salvation in raising Jesus. According to tradition, the service may begin outdoors, under the stars. A fire is lit and is followed into a darkened church. The *Exsultet*, one of the earliest known pieces of Christian chant, pierces the night. It prepares us for an interplay of words and symbols that speak to the mystery that has called us together. Light, water, oil, bread, wine, songs, and prayers—all are declaring a reality beyond what our minds can contain.

We gather as our earliest spiritual ancestors did. We tell the stories of God's people from the beginning. We remember what God has done, and we join to that story our own stories of faith. Our lives become part of that great story.

It begins with creation, the story of our original blessing. It tells us how good it is that we are here. Our universe, our existence, is a wonder. We reverence it. We celebrate it. We are no accident. We can know something about where we come from and where we are going. Our journey is charged with meaning.

> *But the angel of the LORD called to him from heaven, and said, "Abraham, Abraham!" And he said, "Here I am." He said, "Do not lay your hand on the boy or do anything to him; for now I know that you fear God, since you have not withheld your son, your only son, from me." (Genesis 22:11-12)*

It continues with the story of Abraham and his willingness to sacrifice his son Isaac. It is a story that teaches us that we can trust our Creator. We cannot fully understand the mystery of God's call in our lives. We cannot see the complete vision that God has for our good. But we never have to fear God or God's intention for us. Our God is not vengeful. God is not out for blood. When we give ourselves over to God, and to God's will for us, we will be surprised again and again by God's goodness and trustworthiness.

> *As Pharaoh drew near, the Israelites looked back, and there were the Egyptians advancing on them. In great fear the Israelites cried out to the LORD. They said to Moses, "Was it because there were no graves in Egypt that you have taken us away to die in the wilderness . . . ? For it would have been better for us to serve the Egyptians than to die in the wilderness." But Moses said to the people, "Do not be afraid, stand firm, and see the deliverance that the LORD will accomplish for you today; for the Egyptians whom you see today you shall never see again. The LORD will fight for you, and you have only to keep still." (Exodus 14:10-14)*

We see our story in the story of the exodus, too. It teaches us how God responds to our burdens and bondages. God hears our cries and yearnings, and God is at work to liberate us. God wants to free us from slavery and fear, from isolation and addiction, from all the structures of human sin. God wants to protect us from any evil force that threatens us. It is God's power that ultimately breaks every chain.

> *I will sprinkle clean water upon you, and you shall be clean from all your uncleannesses, and from all your idols I will cleanse you. A new heart I will give you, and a new spirit I will put within you; and I will remove from your body the heart of stone and give you a heart of flesh. I will put my spirit within you, and make you follow my statutes and be careful to observe my ordinances. Then you shall live in the land that I gave to your ancestors; and you shall be my people, and I will be your God. (Ezekiel 36:25-28)*

The story continues in the witness of the prophets. They spoke God's words and delivered God's invitations. They were sent when and where they were needed. And we still need them. When we are self-satisfied, they remind us of how far we are from our potential. When we are despondent in our failures, they speak God's healing words and tell us of God's plan to restore our hopes. In our need for redemption, they open our awareness of God's way through life and point us to the path of peace.

*When the sabbath was over, Mary Magdalene, and
Mary the mother of James, and Salome bought spices,
so that they might go and anoint him. And very early on
the first day of the week, when the sun had risen, they
went to the tomb. They had been saying to one another,
"Who will roll away the stone for us from the entrance to
the tomb?" When they looked up, they saw that the stone,
which was very large, had already been rolled back.
As they entered the tomb, they saw a young man, dressed
in a white robe, sitting on the right side; and they were
alarmed. But he said to them, "Do not be alarmed;
you are looking for Jesus of Nazareth, who was crucified.
He has been raised; he is not here. Look, there is the place
they laid him. But go, tell his disciples and Peter that he
is going ahead of you to Galilee; there you will see him,
just as he told you." So they went out and fled from the
tomb, for terror and amazement had seized them.
(Mark 16:1-8)*

We find our story especially in the story of Jesus, the
anointed one, the revealer of a new creation. His story
is the centerpiece, the turning point of human history.
It falls into our history like a rock that falls into a still
pond, sending its energy in all directions of time and
space. It is in his story that God reaches out to us through
one of us.

He was like us in all things but sin. Saint Peter says:
*"He went about doing good, and healing all who were op-
pressed by the devil, for God was with him" (Acts 10:38).* He

preached good news to the poor, freedom to the oppressed. He cured people's illnesses, forgave their sins, and announced a day of salvation. He broke down barriers that kept others apart. He changed people's lives by awakening their spirits. Everything he did taught us what it means to love God with our whole heart and our neighbor as ourselves. Everything he did invited us to live the fullness of life.

And all of that led him to the cross. All of that won him a crown of thorns. He let a sinful world do its worst to him—but, through it all, he remained faithful to his "Abba." Even from the cross he kept loving and caring for others: *"Father, forgive them" (Luke 23:34). "Woman, here is your son" (John 19:26).* He died as he lived: so full of life, freedom, and light, trusting in God who vindicates his servants.

He walked into the wounds of humanity, into the darkness of sin and death, for our sake. He brought God's love and mercy there—and so transformed it all from within. He brought the light that dispels darkness and fear, the power that heals wounds, the grace that redeems. He brought the reconciliation of God and humanity. All became new. And that newness becomes ours.

> *Do you not know that all of us who have been baptized into Christ Jesus were baptized into his death? Therefore we have been buried with him by baptism into death, so that, just as Christ was raised from the dead by the glory of the Father, so we too might walk in newness of life.*

For if we have been united with him in a death like his, we will certainly be united with him in a resurrection like his. (Romans 6:3-5)

POSTLUDE

The Feast

First and last alike receive your reward; rich and poor, rejoice together! Sober and slothful, celebrate the day! You that have kept the fast, and you that have not, rejoice today for the table is richly laden!

—St. John Chrysostom, *Easter Homily*

Something Real

*Then Peter and the other disciple set out and went toward
the tomb. The two were running together, but the other
disciple outran Peter and reached the tomb first. He bent
down to look in and saw the linen wrappings lying there,
but he did not go in. Then Simon Peter came, following
him, and went into the tomb. He saw the linen wrappings
lying there, and the cloth that had been on Jesus' head,
not lying with the linen wrappings but rolled up in a
place by itself. Then the other disciple, who reached the
tomb first, also went in, and he saw and believed; for as
yet they did not understand the scripture, that he must
rise from the dead. Then the disciples returned to their
homes. (John 20:3-10)*

It all began with an experience, which becomes a
message: After the crucifixion, God raised Jesus and he
was seen to be alive. It's in this foundational experience,
this foundational message, that God comes to meet us
and addresses our deepest needs, questions, and hopes.
This becomes the heart of the Christian creed and of
Christian worship.

Churches that observe Lent normally refrain, or fast,
from the singing of "Alleluia" during that season. But
when Easter comes, the fasting is over, and the "Alleluias"
ring out with freshness and joy. The Easter season begins. The mystery is too big, too rich for a day. We must

unpack it, break it open, by searching through the accounts of the resurrection appearances in the gospels and through stories of the early church in the Acts of the Apostles. With those first disciples, we savor our experiences of Christ alive in our midst. For fifty days we celebrate, culminating in the feast of Pentecost. We remember the sending of the Holy Spirit upon the church, and we welcome new outpourings of the Spirit in our own lives.

This is a time of abundance and joy, of feasting and thanksgiving. It is a time to consider our mission to bring the good news to others. We continue to appreciate and explore the meaning of this resurrection faith for us and our world.

One thing it means is that our redemption is not an escape from reality, suffering, or death. There may be other creeds to go to for that, but not this one. You cannot look at the cross and get a message of cheap grace, an easy way out, or a "*deus ex machina*" solution to our problems. Resurrection faith does not offer an escape from this world, but a transformation of this world with its history of sin and suffering. God chooses to redeem us from within. God offers us a path through our life, to a new life.

It means that God vindicates his servants. God shows us that Christ's way is true. Christ's way leads to life. Where do we need freedom and forgiveness? Are we ever locked in fear, grief, or the pain of loss? Where do we need to let go of the old ways, the destructive thoughts and attitudes, that lead us nowhere? Christ's way, his words, his values, his sacrifice, his resurrection—here is the power that overcomes sin, death, fear, or anything that holds us back. Here is the power that heals souls, enlightens minds, and inspires action. Here is the power of God reaching out to us to save.

The witness of those first disciples, our mothers and fathers in the faith, is a reliable witness, supported by grace. It's reliable in its surprising quality. It wasn't what these disciples were expecting. The thought of a crucified messiah would have been an absurdity to them. Yet, that's exactly what they started proclaiming before they could even understand it fully themselves. That's what they believed, because that's what they experienced.

Their message is reliable in the fruit it bears, in its effects on those first disciples and on disciples ever since. We see a radical change in them. These people who were scared, hidden, and scattered after the crucifixion came together in a new way. They moved from grief to joy, from weakness to strength, from fear to courage. They came to know Jesus in a new way, proclaimed him as Lord, and put their lives on the line for his message. They were willing to lose everything for him—that's how free they were from the fear of evil, loss, or death. All was new.

They experienced something real, something that transformed them. And as special and unrepeatable as those foundational experiences are, we, too, as God's people, have access to them.

"This gem of a book challenges us in the spiritual journey to live at the depths—the core of our being. Father Mark, one who knows the human psyche well, leads us to mystical reflections by delving into the Scriptures and applying them to our spiritual life with contemporary examples and fresh insight. He's a gentle guide posing poignant questions that immerse the reader in a personal examen of one's life with God. No matter where you are on your spiritual journey, this book probes, contemplates, and encourages all at the same time!"

— Nancy Usselmann, FSP, author of *A Sacred Look: Becoming Cultural Mystics*

"Are you seeking a spiritual wake-up call or a deeper connection to the Divine? *Journey to Jerusalem: Steps on the Road to Your Soul* by Mark A. Villano is an elegantly crafted invitation to seek the accompaniment of Jesus Christ along your own spiritual path. Challenging in all of the right ways, this spiritual tool is perfect for your Lenten devotional time or any moment where you desire forward momentum in your prayer life."

— Lisa M. Hendey, author of *I Am God's Storyteller*

"Mark A. Villano has the extraordinary talent of writing in a way that captures the interest of those who desire to move closer to Christ. *Journey to Jerusalem* uses Scripture, personal stories, and reflections to help us prepare to meet the Lord with resurrected faith. Are you looking for a fuller, deeper life? Let this book be your companion."

— Ron Rolheiser, OMI, author of *Sacred Fire: A Vision for a Deeper Human and Christian Maturity*

"This book is a retreat. Mark Villano has written a guidebook for the journey. This book will be remembered for its inclusion of the richest sources from Scripture that report eyewitness accounts of having been there."

— Mary Margaret Funk, OSB, author of *Renouncing Violence: Practice from the Monastic Tradition*

"By the end of the journey in reading this book, my soul was awakened with fresh Easter hope. *Journey to Jerusalem* is a rich resource for personal prayer. I know preachers, teachers, spiritual directors and retreatants will also savor these reflections."

— Richard Leonard, SJ, author of *What Does It All Mean? A Guide to Being More Faithful, Hopeful, and Loving*

"Villano has creatively crafted an enriching and nourishing companion. *Journey to Jerusalem* is both practical and inspiring. It is an invaluable resource for individual readers, ministry leaders, parish groups, teachers, catechists, young adults, clergy and more."

— Edith Prendergast, RSC, author of *Grace Abounds: A Call to Awaken and Renew Your Faith*

"The Bible is steeped in meaning drawn from reflection on people, landscapes, events, and the full range of human experiences. In this everyday span of life, God's presence is detected. That is the convincing rationale for Fr. Mark Villano's attractive book of spiritual reflections that take their inspiration from the deep wellspring of biblical imagery. Accessible and inspiring, here is rich spiritual reading open to all."

— Donald Senior, CP
President Emeritus of Catholic Theological Union